From a top cop ar

THE HAPPY HANDGUNNER

Pistol Precision & Power

by
Don Paul
&
David Blaisdell Smith

About the authors: David Blaisdell Smith is a weapons specialist who taught marksmanship for the California Highway Patrol. He has published numerous magazine articles on guns and hunting. Don Paul is the former Green Beret who became a writer after his parachute failed over Panamanian jungles in 1976. He has written eight outdoor survival books.

Copyright: All rights reserved except for bona fide teachers using the parts of the text or all illustrations to save lives. Illustrations may be copied and used freely for instruction or reprint with credits posted.

Gratitude: To the manufacturers of guns, holsters and reloading equipment, who's products help us to remain free and independent.

Editor: Andrew Gribble of Cathedral City.

A.M.D.G.

Prayer: Before we publish, Dave and I bow our heads to acknowledge God, thank Him for his blessings, and ask not that He helps us write, but that we conform to His Word and Will as we do. Lord, we rededicate everything we are to you as this book goes to publication. Our lives are yours, our works are yours, and we acknowledge your Holy Scripture as standing forever. We believe the whole world is under attack by the powers and principalities and that too many of us have surrendered. We repent and want to be called by your Name. May those who read it stand with us as grateful for Your Grace in the founding and blessings of our beloved country. Amen.

Library of Congress Catalog Card Number: 96-67885

Publisher's Cataloging in Publication

Paul, Don, 1937- & Smith, David B. 1936

    The Happy Handgunner---Precision and Power for Handguns / by Don Paul and David B Smith

    p. cm.

    Includes index

    ISBN 0-938263-30-7

    1. Gun Use. 2. Self Defense. 3. Shooting . I. Paul, Don, 1937- Smith, David B. 1936- II. Title

    TS534.5.P38 1995   623.4 '42

                                      QB94-21211

Introducing. . .
QUICK-READER BOOKS by PATH FINDER
New-method, easy-to-read, how-to books.

To write any good how-to book, you have to know your topic thoroughly. That takes years of experience, long hours of reading and special schools. I did all that. I was a Green Beret, a chosen member of Sixth Army's Marksmanship Detachment, a winner of many shooting matches and a good student. Still many people know more than I. David B. Smith is probably the best. He could have become a high ranking officer in the highway patrol- but he doesn't like desks; he likes guns. He spent his career teaching other cops how to shoot. In addition, he reloaded all kinds of ammunition and worked as a gunsmith. We at Path Finder consider ourselves blessed to have found him; he's a super bank of handgun information. I could ask him anything, anytime and he knew the answer immediately. Here, he shares many handgun secrets he learned as well as new developments he discovered.

At Path Finder, we take our best shot at going <u>beyond any other knowledge in a given field.</u> This book contains new developments in handgun precision and power. Our wobble grid measurement is new and presents THE ONLY WAY to determine your safe shooting distance. Our system of Mix n Match is THE ONLY WAY to achieve TOP HANDGUN PERformance. In swift, easy-to-understand detail, you'll discover the newest methods for placing a bullet with precision.

Our text is for speed reading. We designed this text <u>so you get all the information---fast.</u> We really care about your time. Hopefully, we didn't waste even one word. Our electronic scrubbers report:

> If you sub-vocalize but still read at 550 wpm, you should complete this whole book in just under two hours. After electronic scrubbing, we achieved excellent reading-ease. We average under 1.8 syllables per word. Average sentence: Under 17 wds. Average paragraph length: five sentences.

Path Finder books have sold well for more than 20 years. We first invented a way to keep you from getting lost in the woods without using a map or GPS; it was called, <u>Never Get lost. The Green Beret's Compass Course,</u> Over 40,000 copies are in print. After that, we added to our book list and widened our distribution. We published:

Everybody's Outdoor Survival Guide
Great Livin in Grubby Times, our best selling survival book.
Everybody's Knife Bible over 30,000 copies!
24 + Ways to Use Your Hammock in the Field.
CONQUER CRIME, How To Be Your Own Bodyguard.
How To Be a SURVIVOR, Books I & II
CONQUER TERROR, How to Survive the Attack.
THE RIFLE RULES, Magic for the Ultimate Rifleman.

We develop and write about new ideas. We're the innovators who discovered and wrote about:

-A two-ounce, 30¢, wilderness bed for sleeping above ground.

-The light for your hunting knife sheath to light up the ground you walk on.

-How to paint the soles of your outdoor boots so they no longer clog with mud.

-How to use animals to double your survive-ability.

-Green Beret team concepts applied to survival groups so you can enjoy the ultimate life-style outdoors.

-How to sleep in the survival mode. Sitting up to access weaponry, totally camouflaged, with rice on your incoming trail so an intruder will wake you (when the birds flutter).

How to keep poison gas out of your house. How to set up your vehicle for survival in any conditions.

-Never becoming a victim. New and clever ways to beat criminals. **CONQUER CRIME** is so popular, the author appeared on over 250 media shows.

All Path Finder books have gone into multiple editions. Most major outdoor magazines have reviewed our books and our systems have been adopted by many outdoor organizations.

Once you own a Path Finder book, you can order a new, updated copy anytime for half price.

(See the order coupon in the back of this book.)
Check our Site. http://www.survival-books.com

THE HAPPY HANDGUNNER
CONTENTS

INTRODUCTION
1 Why this book? We're angry at what they never told you. Seven deadly handgun sins we must, and do, correct. We add what's new. We fix what's wrong. All-new shooting concepts. Super success in handgun bullet delivery---from a super cartridge, perfect gun and a well trained shooter.

2 Basic Ballistics What happens when you shoot. Three kinds of ballistics and how they relate to bullet placement. Equipment basics.   7

3 Mix 'n Match Loading & Exotic Bullets. How to load your handgun so it does a variety of tasks. Ammunition variety can make you twice as effective. Benefits in long distance shooting, penetration, and stopping power. Why you do it and how.   11

4 Handgun Accuracy. Accuracy defined. How accurate is enough? How to hit by eliminating misses. What sights can do, but don't.   21

MODERN HANDGUNS AND IMPROVEMENTS
5 Choice of Handguns How many buyers wind up with the wrong gun. Power & Type.   Actions and Accessories.   Sixguns & double action revolvers. Slick automatics. How to understand the hierarchy of weapons and its meaning in survival. Handgun bullet placement and limitations.   31

6 Modern Guns for Women. Special gun details and shooting methods to which women <u>must</u> pay attention. Make a personal-perfect choice. Choose type, and caliber according to your size and ability. Solving problems for shooters with fingernails. How barrel length and gun weight hamper women shooters.   41

7 Improving your handgun. Why new guns need improvement. How to make yours perfect. The new fire-lap on pistol bores. Why some additions to handguns aren't worth the powder. Discovering tiny flaws. Stocks (grips), trigger, sights, muzzle brakes & accessories. Handgun preparation for night firing.   47

8 Methods of Carry. Conventional and non-conventional. Discovering non-conventional presentation and its multiple advantages. Holsters. Handbags. Fanny Packs and a variety of discreet ways to carry. Some fast, others faster.   59

YOUR PERSONAL HANDGUN: COMBAT MAGIC

9 Handgun Use. Our new wobble grid determines your safe shooting distance, teaches Phd trigger control and determines how big a caliber you should buy. Shooting positions, Presentation, Target Acquisition and Range. Handgun placement in hierarchy of weapons. Defense shooting plans. Why learning to shoot at night is a necessity.   67

10 Handgun Ammo—-Stopping Power. How to put an immediate end to a gunfight. Learn to build and shoot bullets that stop the fight----and the other side—-cold.   93

PERSONAL SAFETY

11 Handgun Combat Engagement Hollywood has us all fooled; doing things their way will get you killed. Hierarchy in weapons combat. Evaluating chances on the spot and reacting quickly. Key to living. Estimating incoming, power & penetration, range and safety available. Comparing enemy's condition with your own and winning.   101

12 Incoming from handguns. Difference between cover and concealment. Body armor. Psychology and physiology of taking a hit.   113

Bullet and Powder Magic

13 Why Reload? Huge advantages are yours when you make your own. Special ammo fulfills special needs. Savings.   123

14 Making your own ammo. Tools of the trade, some of which add a lot to the ammo you produce. How to put together dream ammunition for your handgun.   127

15 Reloading Safety Make sure your guns are secure. Basic safety pointers for high quality and reliable ammunition. How to cook up high quality and reliable ammunition. We show you how.   137

16 Making your own bullets. Cast and swaged. Dangers of inhaling lead fumes.   141

THE HAPPY HANDGUNNER
Precision and Power For Handguns
by
Sgt. Don Paul and David B. Smith

▢Chapter 1

WHY THESE BOOKS?

> It annoys us that nobody has taught what we consider to be so obvious.

This is not just a handgun book. This is a handgun revolution! Combined, Dave and I have been around handguns for over 100 years. That adds up to <u>thousands</u> of rounds shot, hundreds of pounds of powder dropped into shell casings and dozens of different guns fired. If we had a dollar for every target we punched holes in, we'd be rich.

The comedian Jeff Foxworthy missed this: "You may be a redneck if..."you go to a party full of upper class people, meet another guy like yourself and start discussing handguns." I don't know if we're really rednecks, but we are both plenty perturbed about the lack of progress in the handgun world. Following is a list of "the seven deadly defficiencies."

As it stands right now:

1. Handgun buyers choose for the wrong reasons and often **buy the wrong gun**. That causes reluctance to practice.

2. There has been no **wobble grid** to determine your cone of fire at a distance. When the cone of fire you produce at say, 40 yards, is too large to be effective, you have no business taking shots at targets that far out. Therefore, you don't need a magnum that will shoot so far. Without grid information, gun buyers often purchase too much gun. It will shoot an effective bullet much farther than they can accurately place. Of course, that gun also recoils and goes bang excessively. Therefore, it's heavy, unpleasant to shoot and difficult to carry. Like the majority of handguns, it's stored at home.

Also, trigger pull influence on a shot can't be measured without the wobble grid. Finally, the commonly employed method of finding your best shooting position and practicing now is to burn ammunition. The wobble grid cuts down cost because you can practice without actually shooting.

3. New guns need to be improved after purchase, especially the grip size--for both men and women. Few know how to add grips so the gun can be held correctly. That produces bad shooters.

4. Of all the guns in the world right now, over 90% are loaded with ONLY ONE KIND OF AMMUNITION. **THAT'S WRONG!** Whether for hunting or defense, a handgun has to provide you with versatility. You will be faced with soft and tough targets, short and long distances, and day and night shooting. If your handgun is only a one trick pony and you need a different trick to solve your problem, you don't need a gun as much as a

Bible. Nobody has put out the word about the importance of relative size in handgun shooting. We have no shooting competitions in which that is a scoring factor. **THAT'S WRONG!**

5. Nobody has taught a class on how to deal with incoming. **THAT'S WRONG!** If you are not facing somebody with a handgun aimed at you, you shouldn't even have one in your hand. How then can you be so unprepared for what could easily happen?

6. Few use and nobody has taught--**unconventional methods of handgun carry.** But they are drastically important in a legal system where the first guy to draw and fire goes to prison, and the second guy to draw dies. The way things are right now: Be judged by twelve or carried by six.

7. The concept of adjusting sights **IS WRONG.** Sights don't need to be adjusted, they need to be conformed, and many shooters don't understand this so they never truly find a zero for their handgun.

The above list contains just some of the things that bothered us. What would you do to correct all these problems?

Dave and I decided to put our brains, shooting ability and NEW IDEAS together to bring you information never before in print. To the list above, we would add tricks we know to become a super shooter.

> Fine books do not contain everything authors know.
> Fine books contain what readers need to know.

We will teach you to make or bug high performance rounds---for your much improved individual weapon---and you will shoot with much-improved ability. We want your guns to speak with **ultimate authority!**

Great bullets mean little if you don't know how they relate to weapon performance. A perfect bullet won't do much for you if it comes out of a bad barrel. Improved and super accurate guns mean little if we don't teach you how to shoot them.

TROUBLE WITH NEW GUNS

To create a truly phenomenal shooting result, you need: Ammo, gun and shooter improvement. "Buy this weapon, improve it this way, buy various kinds of ammunition and <u>out-shoot every other gun out there</u>." You'll be able to shoot accurately with a superior gun and better ammo—farther and more precisely-with bullets that have much more influence on any target. For

> **Together, the authors of this book have spent a combined century---over 100 years---in the gun world.** Could we get together and teach you? One or both of us survived in the jungles, worked as a cop, taught others how to shoot, worked as an upgrade gunsmith, carried and fired every weapon, competed and won everything from trophies to medals, shot it out on the street, and read everything in print on the subject of guns and shooting.

years in combat shooting, the focus has been power, speed and <u>accuracy</u>. We need to develop all three. Is this important? Bet <u>your</u> life!

LEARN TO DETECT WOBBLE

Of all the new concepts and instruction we provide in this book, none is more innovative or important than measuring the amount of natural shake you exhibit when you aim. That's why we came up with THE WOBBLE GRID. When your sights shake around you can measure your shooting variation in MOA. That tells you precisely at what distance you can hit. Also, you can copy the page on which we drew the graph and work on different handgun shooting positions **while you note how much your wobble varies.** In the past all we had to go by were the bullet holes you made in the target. But <u>the essence</u> of good marksmanship (or any other sport demanding physical performance) <u>is in tracing error to cause</u>. Our wobble grid allows you to correct your position until you hold tightly enough to shoot super groups.

What else can it do? Teach you trigger control! Listen to this bold statement: <u>Almost everybody</u> disturbs sight alignment when the hammer falls. Some guns even do that when the hammer sideswipes the side of the gun as it strikes. Before the grid, we didn't have a way to <u>measure</u> trigger jerk error. With the naked eye, we dry fire, and it "looks" good. But as if you placed the whole shooting sequence under a microscope, the wobble grid detects the smallest of variations. Without using our grid, there is NO OTHER WAY. Our wobble grid isolates the two most frequent causes of poor shooting. One is wobble; the other is trigger pull. Once detected, correct them and thus eliminate the two major causes of failure in marksmanship. Without the grid, you might find bullet holes on the edge of the target, and only be able to guess what went wrong.

Bullets need to solve particular problems. To be effective, bullets need a certain weight and you may not

---

Some people think of bullets as delivery vehicles for foreign substances. Could we make this happen? A laser guided small caliber round with a sleeping agent? Any near miss on a target would put it down. Years ago, I invented the HAPI bullet-- Hydraulically Activated Poison Injector. Change that now to HASI--sleep inducer.

> This really angers us: Most of the gun magazines and books ignore the problem of incoming. To find out what happens to people who went into combat without considering incoming, visit a police cemetery.

find them at your local store. Why? Because some attorney will sue for millions if a manufacturer produces an exotic round.

DEALING WITH DANGER

People who want life-saving knowledge (cops and military forces) read gun literature in order to stay alive. When they don't get the whole story, they die. Getting shot <u>at</u> is something nobody enjoys thinking about. However, <u>when you fail to prepare, you prepare to fail</u>. In gun talk, don't leave home half cocked. See our chapter on incoming.

We live in troubled times. Both *THE RIFLE RULES* and *THE HAPPY HANDGUNNER* contain the vital gun knowledge you need to survive. Perhaps I could have written these two books on my own. They might have been *good*. But writing with Dave has made these books *great*. I think we've put together the best books Path Finder ever published.

> Almost all police training is inadequate. Some departments require officers to shoot only 30 rounds a few times a year. That places an officer in the field with only the most basic weapon familiarization.
>
> Also, Federal hiring standards make it difficult for departments to disqualify cadets when they can't shoot, so law enforcement shooting standards are now at an all-time low. Like high school test scores, lowered by government to give all students passing grades, many police targets contain no shooting ring scores. Therefore, bad shooters look OK on record---and the department maintains its Federal hiring quotas . . .

Chapter 2

BASIC BALLISTICS

When you pull a trigger, you cause a primer to explode. Gunpowder burns and expands into hot gas, which pushes a projectile down your barrel. Newton's law says, "For every action, there is an opposite and equal reaction." So as the projectile speeds forward, the weapon recoils in proportion to bullet speed and weight. Heavier bullets equal heavier whack to the hand. Faster bullet speed does the same with more smack. Faster speed plus heavier bullet produces whack plus smack, which equals ouch.

In handgun shooting, ouch operates freely because you don't support the weapon with your shoulder. In addition, the gun's muzzle flips upward and shifts in your hand.

THREE KINDS OF BALLISTICS

We call the science dealing with cartridges and projectiles "ballistics," of which there are three types: <u>Interior, Exterior and Terminal</u>. <u>Interior</u> ballistics cover what happens <u>in</u> the gun---the interaction of the primer, powder and projectile while still inside the chamber and barrel. <u>Exterior</u> ballistics is about what happens to the projectile after it leaves the muzzle of your weapon. The forces to consider are gravity and wind. We pay a lot of attention to exterior ballistics when we shoot a rifle because of the long distances involved. But handgun bullets flying under 50 yards away don't have a lot of time to drop or blow sideways. <u>Terminal</u> ballistics, however, are important in handgun shooting. Rifle bullets perform well in the terminal ballistic phase on most targets because they move much faster with more bullet weight. When they smack, they expand like a peeling banana and spin into the target. That's not the case with handguns. Often, pistol bullets don't have enough energy to cause expansion.

Bullet design plays a part, too. Fast moving bullets with full metal jackets sizzle right through; you get over penetration without expansion. Heavier bullets move more slowly and therefore may not arrive on target with enough oomph to cause expansion.

"ADJUST?" SIGHTS

When you **CONFORM** your sights, the strike of the bullet follows the movement of the rear sight. So---rear sight left, bullet strike left. How much? Normally, sights are calibrated in MOA. From our ***RIFLE RULES*** *(*Book I) you know one MOA moves the bullet 1.05 inches at 100 yards. For pistol shooters shooting at 25 yards, one MOA moves the strike of the bullet .2625 inches at that distance. Dave and I really take issue with

---

How fast do pistol bullets go? Did you ever wonder if a pistol bullet can overtake an airplane or car? A 9mm bullet comes out of a barrel moving well over 1,000 fps. One thousand fps (feet per second) is 681 miles per hour.

the gun industry because for over a century, gun experts and manufacturers have told us you have to "<u>Adjust</u>" your sights. That's the wrong word! What they should be saying is, "<u>conform</u>" your sights, and this is why: Imagine a handgun barrel in a rigid vice. You peek through the barrel and see a bullseye. Then you fire. A hole appears where the barrel was aiming. Now you look through the sights. They don't aim where the hole is. What you need to do is to move your sight so it aims at the hole and thus "conforms". Of course, the rigid vice idea is written only to help you understand. Here's how the process goes in real life: 1. Obtain sight alignment. 2. Fire. 3. Observe a hole nowhere near where you aimed. Repeat step 1 and fire again. The new hole is nowhere near the last one you shot <u>OR</u> where the sights were aiming.

How come? Your sights were not aiming at the spot you picked out when the gun fired. Trigger jerks, muscle twitches, eye blinks and perhaps a sudden attack of the St. Vitus Dance have caused me to send lead on it's way to "who knows where"? You may too. So here's how to conform your sights to where an <u>undisturbed</u> barrel points.

First shoot a **meaningful** group. Be careful and hold well. Use the BRASS system; (Breathe, Relax, Aim, Squeeze, Surprise) bring the trigger slowly and straight to the rear, <u>call the shot</u>, then <u>note well</u> where the sights were pointing on the target when the round broke. I'll assume your sights were aligned and natural wobble put you somewhere near the bullseye. On your notepad or the form you can copy from this book, make a mark where you think the round should have made a hole. Then scope the target. If the round isn't where you thought it should be, investigate. What went wrong? With a little practice, the holes in your target will show up where you think they should.

Shoot three. Find the group's center. To do that, draw a straight line from one shot to extend in between the other two. The location where all three lines cross marks the center of the shot group.

Not adjust, but conform your sights vertically and horizontally to move the center of the group where it belongs. Check your owner's manual. I believe you'll find that one MOA click moves the strike of the bullet a quarter inch at 25 yards.

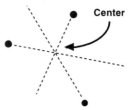

Some sights can be moved with a little screw driver a click at a time. If they are not adjustable, you may have to hit the rear sight with a soft brass drift punch & light weight hammer. Sprinkle some dirt or fine saw dust on the sight you want to move or scratch both sight and gun slightly with a hard knife. Otherwise, you'll never know how much you moved it.

Use the forms we provide in the book to tie your ammunition to performance. Keep good records. If you reload, be deliberate and stay consistent with the same routine every time you assemble rounds.

In rifle shooting, the rifle recoils against your shoulder. If it kicks, it kicks without too much shooter disintegration. But most pistol shooters have a limit for recoil ouch and noise. If a pistol smacks your hand around, you won't be able to hold steady and squeeze.

Don't just go out and shoot; practice with good habits. With conformed sights, a steady hold and your educated trigger finger, all three kinds of ballistics will be tools you can use. Your handguns will speak with ultimate authority.

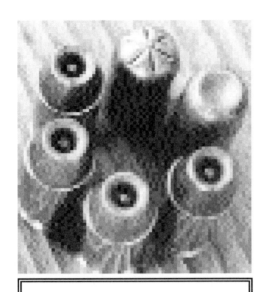

Mixed bullets for a revolver give you more gun-ability. The closed shot shell on the top of the picture delivers a GUARANTEED HIT at close range. Others in the cylinder offer long-range capability and persuade targets to disengage.

Store-bought ammo shoots, but the rounds out of one box only do one trick. Why own a one-trick pony? You need different bullets to perform several shooting chores.

Chapter 3

Mix 'n Match
LOADING WITH EXOTIC BULLETS IN SEQUENCE

If you could inspect ALL of the handguns in the world, you would find that over 90% are loaded with one kind of bullet only. That's wrong. I first advocated mix 'n match in my book, ***CONQUER CRIME***, *How To Be Your Own Bodyguard*. You MUST prepare your handgun to do a variety of chores.

What does Mix and Match mean? Mix means you'll load your handgun with a variety of cartridges for the variety of bullet delivery tasks you may encounter. Some will spread shot. Others such as Hydra-shock hollow points will spread lead after entering a target. Others will speed because they have more powder behind a lighter bullet. Still others will penetrate barricades like car doors and wood fences.

So that your ammo will have approximately the same striking point, try to adjust powder and bullet weight up or down to get close to this result. If you carry special rounds with a different bullet weight for certain situations, find out how they strike and learn to adjust your front blade. What a blessing it can be when you engage a long-range target. You are so far distant that your opponent's cone of fire precludes him from scoring. You, on the other hand, have special rounds to deliver. They will land with extra oomph and you can

> My dad, police inspector B. B. Smith, told me this: Two armed robbers were trying to outrun a two-man Highway Patrol Car. Both passengers made it a running gun battle. Our cop was a good shot with his .38 Special revolver loaded with a mix---158 grain and 110 grain zinc Highway Masters---all of which he let fly.
> The getaway driver failed to make a safe turn and struck a concrete bridge abutment at high speed. Bad driving? Nope.
> Though the officer had aimed for the gas tank, his heavier zincs went low, ricocheted up off the highway under the car and had entered the driver's heel and buttocks. (Thus making it difficult to brake.) Dave

place them with <u>practiced</u> precision.

Some light weight bullets don't produce much muzzle flip in your weapon and therefore shoot low. On the firing range, learn how much you need to raise the blade in the notch to compensate. Count shots when you shoot and adjust for your long-range specials. A problem arises when you get into combat and forget to count shots. If that happens, you won't remember what adjustment to make, which is a great argument for matching by powder and bullet weight to achieve ammo that strikes at about the same height.

Match also means that once you determine a loading sequence for <u>your</u> handgun, you load every magazine and speed loader the same way. If you shoot a revolver, you mark your cylinder (so you can see or feel it at night) and you mark the speed loader the same way. Result--you always have the same sequence rotating.

Mix 'n match is something you can learn with ease. If you buy ammo, trade half of your new box for half of a friend's so you each have a variety. Then test various kinds of cartridge out of your gun. Make changes in front sight elevation for certain rounds to keep bullet strikes as close as possible. Keep records on our performance forms.

WHAT TO MIX

Consider the target-effective result you need to achieve. New targets, each with different circumstances call for a different bullet approach. You're like a doctor, (The same medicine doesn't cure everyone). Solve each

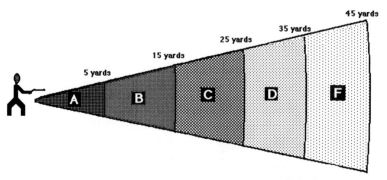

shooting problem by loading your handgun with rounds to solve each different circumstance.

Bullets designed to penetrate at 45 yards will over-penetrate at close ranges, such as A&B. On the other hand, bullets designed to penetrate and expand at close distances will have a lesser effect on targets out at D&F. Hollow points designed to penetrate and open at 25 yards don't do the job if the target has thick skin. That could be a bear with a lot of sub-cutaneous fat (just out of hibernation) or a concrete jungle animal wearing a kevlar vest or heavy wool clothing during winter. Result: You may have sent your customer a bullet designed to penetrate and open at C range, but it acts like an E during the terminal ballistic stage because it slowed down and the nose clogged up with fabric. If that happens, you didn't get the stopping power you required.

Of course, it's difficult to predict the circumstances you may encounter in a gunfight. You never know when, where or how it will happen. If you could predict, you could avoid the fight. With only a handgun for defense, what ammunition would you like to carry?

Most probably, you'll be engaged at under 50 yards. Suppose your attacker is out in the open, nearby and without body armor. For that you need expanding bullets. If dressed in heavy clothing, wearing a bullet proof vest, behind a barricade or in an old domestic car, you need penetration.

The only way to solve a wide variety of problems in the field is to load with several kinds of cartridges, each of which will do a specific chore. Load those various cartridges into your weapon in a sequence according to what situations you believe you'll encounter. Will your first shot most likely take place at close range (A in the diagram)? It can happen; most often, you're surprised. That's one reason a shot shell is first up.

What might other situations be?

a. You might need to punch through an automobile or another barricade such as a house wall. More often than not, people who shoot it out with you when they know you're armed <u>need</u> something to hide behind. A high percentage of shooting incidents involving law enforcement also involve automobiles. New foreign cars penetrate easily. Older domestics (heavy cars) present more protection. We show you how to install Kevlar door panels in our book, *GREAT LIVIN IN GRUBBY TIMES*.

b. You come up against a rifleman and you can't break away from the engagement, so you need a long distance round. Be careful here. Handguns are not for long distance shooting, especially against rifles. If you try a lead exchange with a rifleman, you'll probably lose. (See Engagement) Try a heavy hollow point load. Of course, you need to be a steady long-range shooter.

c. What about survival hunger? You may want a light wadcutter with less penetration to secure small game for food or stop a varmint. (See, *HOW TO BE A SURVIVOR II*).

d.   In an enclosed area in the dark, you may want a round that will respond instantly with shot spread. Try a duplex load to obtain multiple hits. When you use shot loads designed for snakes, birds and small vermin, don't expect great results on two-legged rats. The stopping power just isn't there.

Some rounds you choose to use may be beyond your ability to create on a reloading bench. So order them commercially, then build shoot-alikes (bullets with the same ballistic properties—-trajectory, recoil and velocity) with which you can practice.

> Note: We depict too much variety in both illustrations because we want to show you a wide spectrum. In real life, you might not mix all of these.

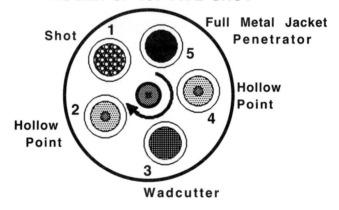

MIXED LOADING FOR RUGER SP-101 FIVE SHOT

MIX? HOW

Once you figure out all the rounds you would like to carry in your cylinder (5 or 6) or in your magazine (7 to 17), you have some basic decisions to make. First, how will you mix them up? Part of the question is multiple choice. Above all, your first consideration should be defense. That's the main purpose of a handgun--- stopping power during a close range confrontation. In snake country, a shot load first is a good idea. But in concrete jungle work, a hollow point or two, followed by a penetrator might be more effective.

Once you have your sequential cartridge pattern developed for your needs, stack your magazines (automatics) or load your cylinders. As mentioned--all mags and speed loaders must be loaded the SAME WAY.

The first round to fire will be the number one load in the sequence, and so forth. Now, suppose you know #4 can solve your problem. If you need to be quiet, cock your hammer and let it down on your revolver a certain number of times so the cylinder presents your barrel with the load you need. On an automatic, you have to pull the slide to the rear smartly the proper number of times to get the ammunition you need into the chamber. Arriving at the proper cartridge silently is method B. Method A

MIXED MAGAZINE FOR MAX EFFECTS

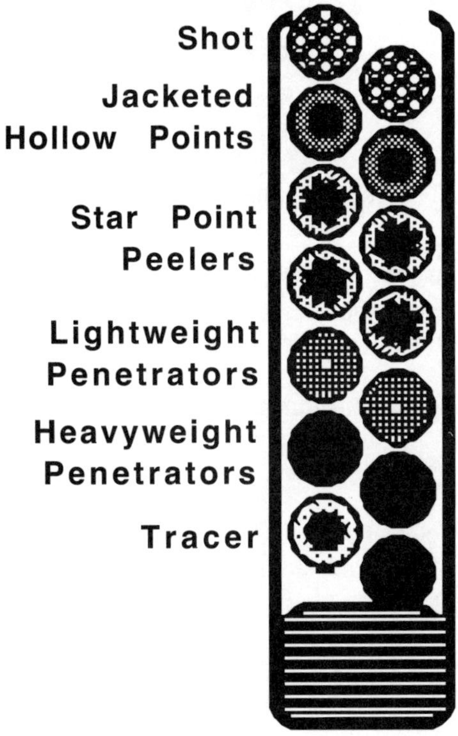

Shot

Jacketed Hollow Points

Star Point Peelers

Lightweight Penetrators

Heavyweight Penetrators

Tracer

says, just keep blasting and counting rounds as you (should) do. When the right load is ready to fire, aim carefully.

ON THE DOWN SIDE . . .

Don't overdo it. Your choices of ammo will depend on how you use your gun. Hunters and fisherman will

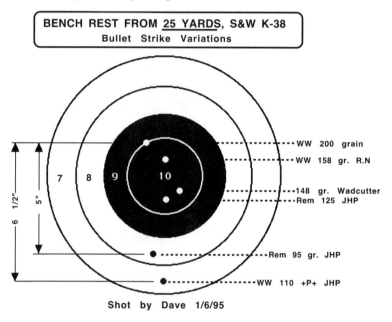

Shot by Dave 1/6/95

FIELD TESTING ON AN OUTDOOR RANGE

Dave shot this bullseye to measure accurately how different bullet weights perform at 25 yards. We scaled his target and copied it precisely on a computer for clarity. It's interesting to note that heavier weight bullets strike higher. Why? More muzzle flip. Note how the longest distance between bullet strikes is six and a half inches at 25 yards. That's not much. In addition, the different bullet strikes are up and down--not really what you would call a miss. Want to make the bullet strike variation negligible? Adjust your sights up or down! Raise or lower the rear sight so the imaginary bullet just over the blade goes in at the middle of your vertical group.

> We test fired a couple of rounds into damp sand. The hand loaded hollow-based wadcutter (reversed with cup forward) expanded to .70 caliber. It out-performed all the factory rounds in expansion. On the right is supposedly the best opener made---the FBI load, a 158 grain lead + P with SWCHP bullet---really no big deal. You can make 'm better than you can buy 'm.

load one way; cops another. If you haven't practiced (100 rounds a month), you probably won't remember to count shots---especially while someone is shooting at you. Therefore, you won't know which round is up. I suggest prayer.

Solve the bullet strike problem at long distance by sighting in for your most-encountered engagement distance. Practice by varying your shooting distance. Then if you have to shoot a long shot with a heavier bullet, know exactly how deep or how high in your notch to hold your blade. Let the gold bead or tritium dot on your front blade guide you into lining up your sights to compensate for the change in bullet strike.

HELPING YOU CHOOSE

Wadcutters are poor choices for long range; they slow down too much. Also, heavier bullets at a long distance drop somewhat, so it could be that the bullet strike rise you get with more muzzle flip gets cancelled out by gravity. How can you be sure? Go to a range. Test fire.

Look at some of the defense loads you can use in a .38 Special. From left to right: Winchester 150 grain (Grn) bullet, 200 Grn bullet, Norma 158 Grn JSW (Jacketed Semi-wadcutter) Super Vel's 110 Grn SP, Winchester 110 Grn JHP (Jacketed Hollow Point). Last three are all Remington's 95 Grn, 125 Grn, and 158 Grn, all JHP's

(SWC)HP = Semi-Wad Cutter Hollow Point
JHP = Jacketed Hollow Point

Rest your weapon and fire carefully. Get perfect sight alignment and squeeze that trigger with the greatest care. Note where the bullet strikes. Perhaps you'll have to raise your blade in the notch to compensate for bullet drop. When you finish, you know exactly what your long distance zero or hold will be.

Mix 'n Match is the answer to almost all possible problems you'll encounter in the field. More than that, it beats firing only one kind of bullet. When you practice, reload carefully and count shots like a pro, you and your handgun can handle any shooting situation with ability others can only dream about.

Chapter 4

HANDGUN ACCURACY

Wouldn't it be great if you could shoot like the Lone Ranger and knock the other guy's weapon out of his hand before he aimed at you? To approach this kind of shooting accuracy, you have to know what handgun accuracy consists of and work your way up through a lot of practice. If you want to become a terrific shot, you first have to understand that <u>there are three kinds of accuracy</u>: Gun accuracy, shooting accuracy, and operational accuracy.

THE GUN

Your handgun can be improved so much, it will place bullets through the center of a coin. You can fire-lap the barrel with a NECO kit, change the sights, work on the trigger and tighten the lockup (auto). We call that "gun accuracy." It has nothing to do with shooter or ammunition---just the gun itself. With the gun in a rest and no wind blowing, a perfect sight picture and a trigger squeeze tender enough to make Michelangelo proud, no outside influence can cause shot group spread. Result: You find out how the <u>gun alone</u> shoots.

Many shooters believe that improving a gun's accuracy is sufficient. Today we have a whole industry of manufacturers and gunsmiths making parts and altering auto pistols to make them match masterpieces. They're usually not the kind of weapon one wants for <u>real</u> combat.

> **Handguns for daily save-your-life must be:
> Compact, safe and malfunction-free.**

Modifications to any auto often cause it to malfunction. Think about blow back for example. Sometimes, it's difficult for the slide to catch up with the rearward movement of the whole gun. Likewise, if you tighten the slide, you increase friction so it doesn't move rearward on the frame as well. Under severe stress and after a quick draw, lightweight triggers often cause the shooter to punch holes through nothing more than air, and they need to thank God the new hole was only through the air. Many others created holey feet.

Anything that adds to your handgun's size will make it more difficult to carry, especially concealed. Muzzle brakes and grip extensions cause your weapon to grow. Some of the custom sights are big enough to catch on clothing, grab in holsters, etc. Safety levers can be a problem too. Only 12% of shooters are left handed. Ambidextrous safeties are of questionable value and just one more gadget to cause a problem at the worst time.

Incidentally, it's <u>imperative</u> that your safety be positive. Whether on or off, you want it to stay that way until <u>you change it.</u> Want a nightmare? Dream about a fire fight in which you can't shoot and you don't know why. What was the horror? You caught a long or protruding safety lever on something during the fight so your weapon was locked up on safe.

Big mushroom magazine release buttons can be bothersome or fatal. "Bothersome" occurs when you discover your magazine hanging halfway out of your pistol butt. During practice shooting, it is extremely bothersome when recoil causes you to lose your index (method of gripping) and you hit the release button by accident, so that a half full magazine lands on the ground. "Fatal" is the result if you accidentally hit the button in the heat of combat. The mag hits the ground and your safety disconnect prevents further firing. With revolvers, oversized cylinder release latches create a similar problem. If you happen to rest your shooting hand thumb on the latch as you fire, **break that habit!** Perhaps glue a sharp piece of metal on it so a recoil tap on your thumb reminds you. Dave writes:

> My dad knew an FBI agent who, during a fire fight, thought his assailant was in front of him. But the criminal germ surprised him by blasting into the room through a door from the agent's right. As he swung his weapon right to get his sights on the guy, he hit the release. So the cylinder flopped open, which caused several cartridges to land on the floor.

You can spend a lot of money making your handgun shoot tight groups. You're far better off to spend all that money on reloading components in order to practice cheaply and become a better shot. Don't tighten up on the weapon, tighten up on your ability. Perhaps spend some money on gunsmithing after you improve.

BECOME AN ACCURATE SHOOTER

You need the ability to aim your handgun precisely and fire it without disturbing that aim. We call that, "shooter accuracy." Shooter accuracy is most often measured with a .22 target pistol on which the grips fit your hand perfectly. In a slow fire situation, you can take your time, line up your sights, <u>squeeeeze</u> your trigger slowly with perfect, increasing pressure, and surprise yourself just as the round breaks. In combat, however, <u>someone else is shooting at you</u>. If you don't point with precision and fire quickly, you may get shot.

Want to get good as a shooter? Practice. Use our wobble grid. Make sure you can shoot without disturbing your sights. Whether slow fire or heat of combat, you can't achieve shooter accuracy unless you develop quick presentation, fast and accurate target acquisition, <u>plus</u> a trained trigger finger.

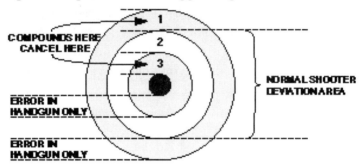

If both you and your handgun are a little off, we get a curious result. The errors can either cancel each other out or compound; it's the luck of the draw. That's why so many gang members carry 9 mm autos. With over a dozen rounds in the weapon, they simply spray the landscape. Sooner or later, their aim will be to the left when the gun shoots to the right. That's all it takes to cause a funeral.

OPERATIONAL ACCURACY

Your ability to create a meaningful hot lead relationship with your target depends on **how well you shoot a particular handgun.** On a scale of ten you may get a perfect gun that shoots like an eight. Perhaps you study the sport and learn to place bullets like a Hollywood hero---so you get a nine. But when you combine this particular gun itself, with you as the

> It doesn't matter how far away you place the MOA wobble grid in determining what your wobble is. Just make sure the size of the grid matches the distance you use. At 25 yards, you need 1/4" squares.

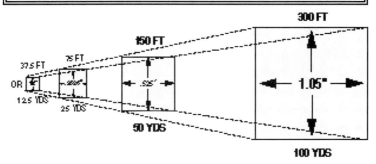

shooter, you wind up with a four. Why? With this particular gun in your (normally great) hands you can't shoot well because of recoil, bad palm fit, etc.

<u>Operational accuracy is the important kind.</u> It's what we strive for. If a hammer spur that is too long stabs you in the web of your hand when you fire, you'll spray lead like grass seed on a lawn. Suppose you are 5'-10" tall. You purchase a .38 Special Ladysmith from Smith and Wesson. Great choice. But women who are tall normally have long fingers. Long fingernails make the situation unbearable. The Ladysmith grip is small, and without fatter grips, you won't be able to maintain your hold on the weapon during firing. Result: After your first shot, you start punching holes in the horizon.

Where do certain kinds of bullets shoot? Muzzle flip can change your zero. You need to know exactly how each round performs and adjust your vertical sight alignment accordingly. A center-of-mass zero is the best. For the distance at which you'll shoot most often, adjust your sights precisely so the bullet goes into the target right over the front blade.

Try to adapt your firing practice to what you will encounter in the field. Don't conform your sights for a 6 o'clock hold or you'll have to remember that the bullet strike is 6 inches high at a certain distance. In the heat of a hunt? I don't think so. I used to hunt bear behind a pack of hounds. Sooner or later, the bear would climb a tree---usually a mile or so away, and I had to hike through Oregon's coastal range. I couldn't carry a rifle or a bow through all that woods and brush. Handgun was the only way. Most of my shots were downhill at 25 yards and I had time enough to aim.

You may not be so lucky. The animals in the concrete jungles shoot back. In law enforcement or self defense, a quick first shot may save your life. Practice for it. You and your handgun can provide some *GREAT LIVIN' IN GRUBBY TIMES*. (Survival book title by Path Finder $12.95).

Here's our wobble grid. Use it from various positions to measure your ability to hold your weapon steady.

The numbers on the grid increase in all directions from zero/zero at the center. Add the numbers left and right as well as up and down to find out how large your wobble is. Convert the measured wobble information to bullet flight error at a <u>certain distance away</u>.

Don't take shots which fly too far wide and therefore miss. When you miss, all you do is disclose your position. Enlarge or shrink the grid on a copier so the size is exact for the distance at which you will shoot. For example: At 25 yards, one MOA is equal to a quarter inch.

Then use the grid a second time to measure sight alignment disturbance when you pull the trigger. Are you jerking?

The military <u>needs</u> this information. During the Korean conflict, we expended 10,000 rounds for each enemy hit.

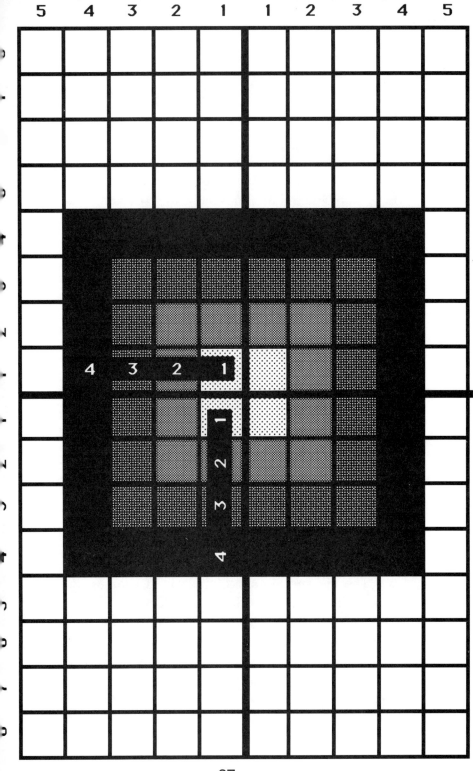

SHOOTING ACCURACY

> The key to **all** good shooting is: First: Align sights. Second: Cause aligned sights to line up on target. Third: Cause the weapon to fire **without** disturbing the sight alignment.

Shooting misses occur because:

A. The weapon is inconsistent. Some auto pistols have sloppy barrel bushings and slides (government .45's were this way). So the barrel actually points all over. Remember: Small fractions of an inch cause misses.

B. You can eliminate all the misses caused by ammunition if you put rounds together that are perfectly suited to your handgun. You can also reduce powder charges or bullet weight so you shoot within your comfort zone---which is also the scoring zone. Once you have good ammo coming out of an accurate gun, learn to shoot (C).

C. Work carefully and diligently on your shooting ability. Align your sights properly. Learn to be consistent and follow the BRASS rule when shooting (see *THE RIFLE RULES*).

With good grips, hold on to your weapon so the barrel alignment with your forearm stays the same. No trigger jerks! When all is said and done, you become an expert marksman by eliminating all the causes of misses.

FINDING YOUR ZERO

The measure around a circle is in degrees--360 of them to be exact. In each of those degrees, we count 60 MOA, **M**inutes **O**f **A**ngle. That's how we measure bullet deviation and adjust handgun sights. Therefore, each click on your sights usually represents one MOA. The most frequently asked question is: Which way do you conform sights to move the strike of the bullet?

The strike of the bullet follows the direction toward which you move the rear sight.

ADJUSTING FOR DISTANCE WITH FRONT SIGHT WALK-UP

Close   **Farther**   **Farthest**

> The system for shooting at long distance targets has been, "hold over". They want you to aim above your target. That is **really wrong**. Holding over takes your target out of view. Whether hunting or in combat, your target will probably move. Dave has a much better system for shooting at targets far away: The dot on the front blade measures precise height as you raise it in the rear notch. Elevating your blade in the rear notch makes your bullets reach out to a longer range with much better accuracy than you get with hold-over.

So, at 50 yards, when you come one click up, you can expect your next round to be a half inch higher. The same goes for windage. If you move your rear sight one click to the left, the bullet will move one MOA to the left also. With sights conformed, ammo perfectly loaded, a weapon that shoots decently straight, and shooting ability to make it all come together, others will never out-shoot you.

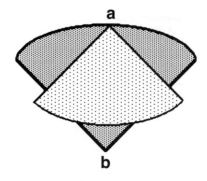

OVERLAPPED SHOOTING RANGES during a gun fight

> Shooter **b** has an advantage over **a** because he/she shoots more accurately. Once you become an accurate shooter, take advantage of your ability by shooting at long distance. That way, you stay out of range.

As soon as you can shoot and handle the recoil, move up to a caliber that will out-range most others. To survive, you'll need to place bullets more accurately than others who may shoot at you. When you can do that, then you can shoot and hit from far away, while others against you can come only close. That insures your relative safety.

> Senator Ted Kennedy pushed hard for the Brady Bill. He shouted, "A pox on anyone who calls this weapon a sporting firearm." Comedian Dave Letterman had a better idea: A gun-type law that says you have to wait five days before you can buy a politician.

Chapter 5

MODERN HANDGUNS

In *GREAT LIVIN' IN GRUBBY TIMES,* you learned that pistols should be your last choice in survival weapons because they are difficult to learn to shoot. Handguns are expensive, have limited range, and with few exceptions are third in the hierarchy of weapons. They don't have the power of shotguns or rifles. But handguns are concealable; and require only one hand to shoot. That's convenient if your other hand is driving a vehicle or is otherwise occupied.

Think of handguns for one of two uses: Hunting and defense. For hunting, you can go with a long barreled revolver in a hip holster. I hunted black bear for years with a Ruger single action .357 magnum revolver. To get a better hold on a bullseye during practice, I adjusted my sights for a six o'clock hold. Bad mistake.

When I faced the bear, I held high on his sternum. The round went in higher of course. I thought I had missed and made him mad; he certainly showed no sense of humor as he came out of that tree with a terrible attitude. The rounds I shot were semi-wadcutters in front of a powder load that made them depart the muzzle at 1400 fps. I shot again. My sights looked good as the round went off. I knew for sure I put that round somewhere in the bear's back but I got no reaction. Later on, after a horrific fight with the dogs, the bear rolled over and expired. Dr. Don's field autopsy revealed cause of death to be from sudden weight gain (hot lead). Both rounds had hit well in good places on the bear's body, but hadn't expanded to cause much of a wound cavity.

> Sight picture methods here are A, the six o'clock hold and B, the dead-center, or, center-of-mass hold. It's best to adjust your sights so the bullet goes in right over the front blade (B). From what distance? At a distance from which your wobble will <u>NOT</u> cause a miss. Shorter distance shots often punch a hole in the target slightly higher.

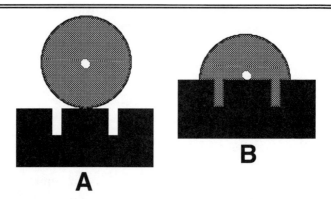

What's to learn from this? Make sure your bullets land on target with enough energy to 1, penetrate and 2, open up to create a devastating permanent wound cavity. Zero your handgun so it places bullets right over the blade as in B, not A. Install a dot on your front sight so you can easily elevate the front blade and thus shoot from a distance.

WHAT KIND?

Choose from autos or revolvers—-either double or single action. Double action means the hammer is activated (to the rear and forward) by a simple pull on the trigger. It's harder to hit anything that way, but you get a first round off faster. Revolvers normally hold only six rounds (.22's are an exception) and you reload a double action all at once by flipping open the cylinder

> Revolvers are best---but only for the first six rounds.

and pushing down on the ejection rod. A speed loader enables you to drop six new rounds quickly. You don't have to wait until you've emptied the gun to do that; anytime before is great. If you mix 'n match, you'll have special rounds in your speed loader. Some choices are: Jacketed hollow points for maximum wound cavity, shot loads for snakes or birds, a duplex load for close distance, and a penetrator to go through a barricade.

Single actions have to be cocked by hand before you shoot them. That's OK while hunting, but for defense it's cumbersome. If you're tactical, single actions make far too much noise. Cock the hammer back and it tells

> For the revolver purchaser who won't be practicing much, single actions have some advantages. For the outdoors person and horse rider, single actions never have a trigger pulled accidentally (bucking horse). Think of the safety; if you don't deliberately cock the weapon, it won't fire. Single actions are smaller and lighter, even though they chamber a powerful round. SA cylinders never get bent out of line like their double action cousins. You only have to learn one kind of trigger pull. Because of longer barrels and the SA (light) trigger pull, these guns shoot more accurately, even from the hip. *Dave*

> Not many single-action, fast draw artists have stood on holy ground, but more than a few have holey feet.

your adversary where you are. With the weapon holstered, a la Western Movie, you're supposed to draw, cock the weapon with your thumb and shoot. The other way is to hold the trigger down while you fan--flip the hammer down by slapping it with your non-gun-hand palm. Fanning is definitely a very close range technique. At longer ranges, you will spray lead all over.

Loading singles with new rounds one by one isn't my idea of speed. The combat exception comes with a system I published in *THE AMERICAN HANDGUNNER ANNUAL* 20 years ago. You can always keep a single action fully loaded if you fire and then half-cock to bring the empty brass in line with the loading port. The gun clicks as you rotate the cylinder while the hammer is in the half-cock position. With a little practice, you'll be able to rotate to an empty cylinder, eject and refill it, all without looking. It's a great skill to have. With the loading gate open, a shove on your ejection rod will empty that cylinder, which you quickly refill. When you reload as you fire, you keep your single action revolver 100% ready.

No matter what handgun you choose to own, learn how it works---loads, revolves, slides, etc, in the dark. You need to learn to operate everything by feel---and thus reload revolvers, clear jammed automatics, release safeties, etc. without looking.

We see an increasing number of automatics on the streets. When we say auto to describe pistols, we mean autoloader, not auto shooter. Autos not only have more firepower than revolvers; they also reload easier and

> Incidentally, over 40% of Los Angeles is now foreign born. Political groups there put a lot of pressure on the police to keep "their people" safer. Therefore, I'll just bet the department is not using any super-expander rounds. That's bad news <u>for all of us</u>. The 9 mm. puts out over 1200 fps (really speedy), and a non-expander bullet will whistle right through a target. If you and I happen to be out on the same street on which the shooting occurs, we could get hit with a wild round. The same danger holds true for gangbangers who may be using military ammunition. A FMJ (Full Metal Jacket) round is dangerous because it ricochets.

more naturally. Even with a speedloader on a double action revolver, you need your shooting hand to drop six rounds in a cylinder. But you maintain your shooting grip on an auto while you bring your non-shooting hand towards your shooting hand, which is a natural move. Learn to position your magazine on your body so that it's ready to jam into your pistol without having to fumble around with it in your hand.

Auto handguns now come in **SAO, DA**, and DAO. Don prefers SAO (Single Action Only). You carry SAO's in one of three modes---<u>hammer back, safety on</u>; hammer half cocked, round in chamber; or hammer down on empty chamber. Underlined is best for business. Dave likes DA's because they fire the first round with a quick trigger pull (close range), and thus deliver the first bullet in any exchange. After that, DA's fire single action because the slide cocks the hammer for you. **D**ouble **A**ction **O**nly handguns require the shooter to squeeze the trigger hard enough to get the hammer back each time. That's terrible.

With SAO's, **S**ingle **A**ction **O**nly autos—-such as AMT's and military .45's, you put a round in the chamber, cock the hammer back and flip the thumb

> More bells and whistles than you can count. A real "space gun." We named it that--not for the way it looks, but for the huge space it occupies.

safety, a condition we call cocked and locked. A simple thumb wipe puts seven rounds at your disposal. The Star PPD model or a Colt Officers model is a miniature version---small and handy. The velocity of the .45 ACP is not tops, but the diameter of the bullet delivers real punch. Want to improve it a lot? Get a bullet mold for casting a .45 ACP pointed round out of pewter. You shoot a lighter bullet (146 grains) which is much harder than lead. Result: High velocity in the 1,200 fps range with super penetrating ability. It goes right through a 1/16th inch cold rolled steel plate.

Autos require maintenance. If you don't clean and lubricate them, they have a nasty habit of "failing to feed" which means not smoothly ejecting an empty casing and loading another live round. That's why so many enforcement officers <u>carry more than one handgun</u>. You should too.

For most shooters, the big magnums are a poor choice. After 20 rounds from one of the big magnum pistols, I start loosing trigger control. Likewise, pistols chambered for rifle cartridges have a limited use for big game in terrain where carrying a rifle would be near impossible (West Oregon's coastal range mountains).

Powerful pistols are big, heavy, and cumbersome. Big caliber heavy pistols are often kept in storage out of reach. Ask yourself: Would I rather have your small weapon with me often, or store a heavy, combat hog at home where it's unavailable when I need it?

The same holds true with power. Hitting with a .22 round is far better than a miss from a .44 Magnum. A heavy bazooka handgun often causes a shooter to miss because it has too much muzzle blast and kick. So the shooter jerks the trigger or pulls his arm down in anticipation of the heavy recoil. The rule is: **Never buy more handgun than you can shoot with comfort and accuracy.** If Israeli hit teams use .22's, you should think about it also. Just fire more shots.

Law enforcement officers should lean toward autos to match the firepower on the street. Magazines hold more and jam into the gun faster than the speed loaders for revolvers. Practice is required, however, but many departments just don't have the budget to furnish officers with enough ammo to keep them proficient. To keep up without actually burning powder, work on magazine changes and use our wobble grid for dry firing.

In some automatics, certain rounds don't slide well up the bullet ramp into the chamber. Without maintenance, autos also malfunction, a problem which

---

In sort-of Biblical terms:
Many buy; few practice.

most often requires two hands to clear. Finally, autos spit cases all over. Have a hot brass case bounce off a windshield and burn your skin. That's certainly a distraction. Revolvers don't give you those kinds of problems.

What happens if your handgun misfires, or worse, you get it taken away from you. How do you prepare for something like that? **Carry a back-up!** Dave believes it's best if your back-up and your main handgun are the same caliber. The exception would be a back-up shooting rimfire, where the secondary ammunition is so easy to carry. Don likes the concept of range overlap and therefore, tactical superiority. To achieve that you carry two different guns, one of which is a long range shooter. Perhaps your primary is a .357. Both those handguns reach way out and make your influence felt. In that event, you can carry a palm back-up in a lighter caliber---something for close range work.

What caliber? Opinions on caliber and smack vary. What is good for some people may not be for others. Although .25 and .32 ACP autos are in common use, they just don't have the smack for defense. You can choose from any of these: .380 ACP, 9 X 18, 9mm., **.38 Spl.**, **.357 Magnum**, .40, .44 Special, 45 Long Colt, or .45 Auto. We leave out the .41 and .44 magnum calibers. They pack too much smack to be shot accurately by average people. Dave's dad calls them "44 mangelems."

<u>Don't disregard rimfire</u>. Two ways to be stocked for survival are: A. Buy a centerfire handgun, get the dies, presses, bullets, and powder, and build a basic inventory of 500 rounds. For more power, go for the .357 Magnum. It will shoot .38 Special's, plastic and wax training loads, shot, and hot Magnum rounds. B. Purchase a .22 magnum; buy 500 rounds which take up

the space of a quart of milk. Some .22 revolvers come with an extra cylinder chambered for the .22 Winchester Magnum which has a muzzle velocity of over 2000 fps, and delivers over 200 ft. lbs. muzzle energy. That's better than a standard velocity .38 Special cartridge. One caveat, however. A .22 mag out of a derringer won't get going much faster than a .22 LR. If you want real zip out of a .22 mag auto, get a six inch barrel and gas channeling for trouble free action.

Longer sight bases found on long barrels provide more accuracy. In addition, long barrels give powder more time to burn and produce bullet velocity and stopping power. Figure on losing about 25 fps for each inch of barrel less. So a four inch barrel might shoot 100 fps slower than a six inch. Another notable advantage: Longer barrels produce less muzzle flash.

Watch out, though; longer barrels on handguns make them easier to take away, so if you are timid about shooting, buy a gun with a shorter barrel. All factors considered, just over three inches is all-around best.

Handguns lack power at long range, and require skill to shoot, but they can be your saving grace in grubby times when no other weapon is available. They conceal easily, are convenient to carry and are fast in presentation. With home built loads, they can deliver a much-improved variety of bullet.

Become totally familiar with any handgun you will use. Dry fire it. Load magazines, and clear obstructions while blindfolded so you can operate in darkness.

Spend the time to learn exactly how to shoot the handgun of your choice. Indoor ranges have become popular. Get instruction if you need it. After you learn, you and your handgun can keep your freezer full and your house safe.

PISTOL CARTRIDGE: LOADING AND SHOOTING DATA

LOADING DATA

a.

b. LOT ID# color/letter   Caliber   Case: Mfg. Type & OCL   Date / time

c. Bullet: weight/kind   Powder & weight   Cast bullet data
   Primer Crimp
   NOTES

PERFORMANCE RECORD

d.

e. Handgun   Mzzle Velocity   Barrl length   Range   Energy @ range

f.

g. Ext. ballistic influence   Penetration? Slug Expansion? Target Type

h. Shots since cleaning?   Second group distance change

j. Point of Impact / Zero?   Support?   Flyers?   Sight Adjustment? Windage/Elevation

k. NOTES

Sight Configuration for this group

Stance P K S Offhand
Muzzle Flip MOA:____

Copyright release on this form for your personal use. Copy about 50 of these and have them spiral bound into your personal reloading book. Top lines are for loading data, bottom five lines and target are for performance.

> Little guns seldom solve big problems.
>
> Dave

Chapter 6

MODERN GUNS FOR WOMEN

When a woman walks into a gun shop anywhere and tells them she wants to buy a gun, they often ask, "What do you want it for?" Perhaps she will answer "Protection." Then the store clerks will offer suggestions on what might do the job. Even so, the gun she buys is frequently the wrong handgun for her individual needs. Contrary to that, men buy guns too big. I've done hundreds of call-in media shows on **CONQUER CRIME,** and many have called to discuss the .44 mangl'ems they keep for home protection.

When buying pistol protection, these are the criteria to use. Will you shoot a lot? If so, economics may compel you to choose a .22, which doesn't do much to stop a crazy person unless you score multiple hits. Of course, if you practice, many multiple hits will be easy to place. Israeli hit teams--well trained and highly professional--carry a light caliber. Small caliber---less noise and easy suppression. Small gun---light weight and easy concealment.

What about caliber? How big are you? Strong women may handle a .357 magnum. Can you carry the weight of a heavy gun with you <u>conveniently</u>? If not, you may get into the bad habit of leaving your gun at home. Will the gun you intend to buy fit in your purse, or better, your fanny pack? In her book, *ARMED AND FEMALE,* Paxton lists various weapons by intimidation factor. Almost all rapists are aware that a big hole in the end of the muzzle means a big hole in their body. But that's intimidation by sight when they can see it. Many rapists attack after dark. If you carry a short barreled .22, the noise from the first round you fire will shake up anybody. That's intimidation by sound. Finally, though, think of the best intimidation possible, by feel. With a .38 Special shooting hollow-cupped wadcutters loaded cup-first, the sight, the noise and the wallop will scare everyone.

While all of the above criteria have some import, the major question you have to answer in making a caliber choice deals with <u>FPE (Foot Pounds Energy) at shootable range.</u> First, let's define shootable range.

AT WHAT DISTANCE ACCURACY?

Given that you can aim and hold that aim true while the hammer falls, determine this: How far away can you shoot accurately enough to produce consistent hits. That's why our wobble grid is so important. When a woman walks into a gun store to purchase a weapon, the grid provides critical information. What's her wobble? The amount of wobble is <u>the</u> one factor which defines shootable range. If the wobble grid tells you long range shots will miss, why buy a .357 mangl'em that will shoot a far distance? Also, consider this: Wobble always increases during high stress. What else might cause wobble to increase? Handgun weight. Heavy handguns cause more wobble because of muscle fatigue. Additionally--big gun recoil and noise often create trigger jerk--which is death to accurate shooting.

You <u>are not allowed to miss!</u> No matter what the cause, sight misalignment or wobble, any deviation more than 16 minutes means you shouldn't take a shot farther away than 50 yards. If that be the case, why buy a big caliber with a long barrel? ALL YOU REQUIRE IS A SMALL CALIBER / SHORT BARREL TO DELIVER ENOUGH FPE WITHIN THE DISTANCE AT WHICH YOU CAN HIT.

FPE = FOOT POUNDS OF ENERGY @ TARGET

FPE is a product of bullet velocity times weight, so more FPE also means more recoil. We reduce recoil by making the gun heavier. But with a heavy (big) gun, concealability and carry capacity diminishes and of course, wobble increases.

So the absolute rule for women who buy guns is: Don't buy a gun that shoots beyond the effective distance at which you can hit. "Effective" means with penetration and expansion. When a woman owns a gun she can shoot effectively ONLY AT SHORT RANGE, she gets several benefits. 1. Light weight. 2. Concealability. 3. Confidence.

Remember from the accuracy chapter---what we're after is **operational accuracy.** The gun, itself, may be super accurate. Custom made ammo may be precision stuff. You may even be a decently trained shooter. But you may not be able to shoot this particular weapon. You have to assess your abilities carefully before you buy too much gun. If you <u>do</u> buy too much gun, you have a remedy: Download for it. The .357 accepts .38 Specials.

REVOLVER OR SEMI-AUTO?

For a first-time gun buyer, we recommend revolvers. Revolvers are reliable. Autos are complex and moody. They also require expertise, which means plenty of practice. Consider this also; ladies with long fingernails have a hard time shoving shells into an automatic's magazine.

GRIPS

In her book, *ARMED AND FEMALE,* Paxton writes, "The next and perhaps most important aftermarket customizing that must be done to almost every revolver, and especially to a woman's gun, is the installation of the proper-size grips." To which I add: Absolutely. If you don't make the grip fit your hand, you won't be able to hold on after firing just once.

BARREL LENGTH

Long barrels give you more accuracy because they support a longer sight base. Short barrels, on the other hand, are more compact, easier to carry, and of course, harder to grab. But the slightest error with a short barrel is often three times as bad as the same error with a longer barrel.

Also, short barrels don't allow the powder enough space in which to push the bullet up to speed. You can fix that if you reload; use a faster burning powder and a lighter bullet.

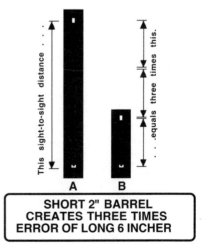

SHORT 2" BARREL CREATES THREE TIMES ERROR OF LONG 6 INCHER

SIGHT SYSTEMS

Laser sights can be extremely helpful when training because you can see the dot move on our wobble grid-- either as a result of excessive wobble or jerky trigger snaps. Call B-Square at (817)-923-0964. For combat shooting, we're less enthusiastic. Unless you check your batteries daily, you could rely on sights that won't power up. Also, lasers add bulk to your weapon. Dot telescopes are also bulky. Worse, they require time in which to locate a target. So the standard, old, notch and blade sight is our favorite. But the way they come from the factory, they need improvement.

~~Look~~, no, <u>stare</u> at the spaces between the blade and the notch on both sides. In the illustration, the sights at C were misaligned by a computer nudge of just one pixel. It's not that easy to see. In real life shooting, you have to <u>stare</u> at the front blade and make sure you have an even distance on both sides of the blade. With a file, widen the notch in the rear sight to cut down on your target acquisition time. In the next chapter, we'll show you how to drill your sights and insert our illuminated dot system. If your sights don't have dots like these, your handgun is <u>only</u> operational during daylight. You may as well put a sign on your door: "Attackers and rapists not allowed after dark." If you'll be taking long shots or using various ammo blends in your weapon, the dots enable you to adjust. You'll be able to raise the front blade to shoot higher (farther away).

A
Dot not centered on blade

B
Which of these two sights is misaligned?

C
How much? Answer in text.

In these tough times, more women need to carry a handgun, (see my books CONQUER TERROR, How to Survive A Terror Attack & CONQUER CRIME, How to Be Your Own Bodyguard). When you know you can hit from a certain distance, choose the caliber and bullet that will smack and destroy a target within your shooting range. You need enough kinetic energy to make the round penetrate **and** open up inside your target's body. Look in the tables found in most gun manuals to find that caliber. Then, keep on practicing. When you carry a gun you can shoot, you'll exude confidence. That's an attitude street thugs will read like a book. Thus, you'll be safe.

Chapter 7

IMPROVING YOUR HANDGUN

Many people buy expensive cars they can barely afford. And then--surprise! "I also have to buy insurance and gas." Gun buyers frequently purchase weapons the same way. They spend their last buck on the gun, and have nothing left for cleaning equipment, add-ons, improvements, etc.

New out of the box, handguns leave a lot to be desired. Some improvements you can make are obvious. Although everyone's hand is a different size, the manufacturer only makes one size grip. The sights are often inadequate. Screws and grips aren't tight and some safeties flip-flop. Husky men with large hands sometimes experience this: Recoil flips the muzzle up and the hammer stabs the shooter in the hand between the thumb and trigger finger. Solution: Ask a gunsmith to cut off part of the hammer and grind it smooth. A few trigger pulls are atrocious. You can do a lot to improve your handgun and the result of doing so will be: You can out-gun most of the others <u>with</u> whom you shoot, as well as <u>those against</u> whom you shoot. That's good life insurance.

First, customize your weapon so it doesn't do anything detrimental during the most critical times. When you buy a new handgun, you need to look at it, sight it, feel the balance, consider the weight, and then touch it all over to see if it has any rough edges. Sharp edges catch on things or dig into a shooter—-which can destroy your ability to shoot. Rough surfaces on moving parts, burrs on the back of the handgun frame, rear sight so narrow that finding the blade is like an Easter egg hunt---likewise prevent you from shooting.

Fire-lapping is a great handgun improvement for steady handed shooters. Fire-lapping does this: It removes high spots inside the barrel and mirror-polishes the bore surfaces. Therefore, your weapon doesn't foul as easily. That could be significant. In a normal

---

Dave went out on the range with a .357 and tested it before and after fire-lapping. To make the test fair, he used a rest both times. After fire-lapping, his group was reduced to almost half the size.

You may not shoot well enough now for it to make a difference, but if you ever have to shoot long range with tight sights, a fire-lapped barrel makes a world of difference.

shooting event, a handgun's barrel will foul with copper, lead and other crud. When that happens, it starts throwing flyers, rounds that don't come close to staying with your group. Even though your first rounds (out of a clean bore) fly true, later ones take off like Star Trek-- out there where nothing has gone before. In combat, it could mean an unexplainable miss. Fire-lapping costs about $100; the extra insurance and ease of cleaning makes it a prudent thing to do.

Think about your eyes. Handgun flash can cause night blindness. Learn to close one eye hard while shooting in the dark. Reduce muzzle flash. Either reload ammo with a fast burning powder so most of the burn stays inside the barrel or buy a gun with a long barrel. Does your handgun bounce like a wild bucking bull? Cutting a muzzle break in the end of your weapon to reduce muzzle flip stops that. However, it increases the noise level. Perhaps you solve the noise problem with electronic ear protection. You can now get mickey mouse ears which let in ordinary sounds, but block out the big bangs. Of course, if you work in law enforcement, you don't get to put the ears on when action erupts. No matter. When you are in the heat of combat, you won't hear much anyway.

THINGS THAT <u>UN</u>-IMPROVE YOUR HANDGUN

I buddied-up with gunsmith Daniel Norwood at a Dallas SHOT show, who taught me this trick. Many clean their weapons with metal cleaning rods. If one tiny piece of metal breaks off and slips down behind the lift plate, it will jam the weapon at a critical time and leave you defenseless. Use a magnifying glass after cleaning and make double sure you're not guilty of sloppy housekeeping.

Speaking of gunsmiths... Some have bad days, just as all professionals do. Worse, you can encounter some who never had a good day, which includes most amateurs. Be advised that sear and safety angles and clearances are measured in thousandths of an inch. Bad adjustments can make your gun inoperable. Other adjustments can make your gun a lethal liability. All throughout the history of firearms, hair triggers have sent bullets into many unintended directions. Another widow-maker for law enforcement officers is excess oil on the firing pin of an automatic. People go to work every day with the weapon in a holster, barrel down. So excess oil on the firing pin slowly drips down—-onto the primer of the round in the chamber, which makes it a dud. Pull the top round out of your magazine regularly and replace it with a new one. Use Pro-Tec grease or rig on your firing pin. No drips.

Other things not to have on your handgun are what some refer to as transfer bars. They transfer money from your account to the manufacturer's. In some cases, they actually make the gun perform worse. One good example: A mushroom button can cause an accidental release of your magazine. It's most important in a slug fest to know when your magazine will empty. It's also a good idea to change magazines early—-before they empty. But an accidental release—-**no way!**

Dave's general law of gun improvement says:

Most gun improvements for special use are death for the day-to-day business gun. Trigger shoes for target guns, scopes for speed shooters, special holsters for quick draw artists, thumb rests on revolvers which prohibit speed-loader access, and other hot-shot improvements often cause a business gun to malfunction just when your life depends on it.

On the subject of release, **don't buy** a handgun with a magazine disconnect safety. Such a device keeps the gun inoperable when the magazine is not engaged in the mag well. Translation: Hit the release button accidentally, get something lodged improperly in the well, or fail to insert a new mag correctly, and all you have in your hand is a club. It's much better (not safer, however) if you can fire the weapon with the magazine removed because you can then change mags with a round in the chamber. If the guy on the other side of the shoot-out is proficient, he knows the sound of a magazine hitting the deck and he may come out from behind cover. Even if you lose all your magazines you can load and fire one round at a time. (How do you aim with only one round in the chamber? Very carefully.)

IMPROVING YOUR GRIPS

The verb, *to index* (a handgun) means *to grip* it firmly and properly. It's also a noun. In order to index correctly, a handgun's grip needs to be even pressured against the hand on all sides of the weapon. On a stock too small for your hand, you'll have a slight space where your hand can't index the weapon firmly. Then recoil will move the weapon in your hand, thus destroying your index---and therefore your sight alignment.

Although good grips will absorb recoil somewhat, the main function is to provide the shooter with a secure index. That's why most serious shooters replace originals grips with new sticky rubber ones (Paxton Quigley recommends Pachmayr grips for women). Some handguns come out of the factory with decent grips on the sides, but without gripping material on the front or rear of the gun. Quick solution: Remove the grips, wrap the whole stock with wet or dry sandpaper, and re-attach the grips to the side. One additional police note: Sticky rubber grips catch on clothing. A hip holster covered by a coat that hangs up on the butt of your handgun will absolutely blow your cover.

Mother of Pearl is a grip no-no because it will slip like hot butter when your palms get sweaty. No custom

Almost all stock grips are poor and won't fit your hand. To find out if your new grips fit at the store, bring your gun and try them on. The best way to test the grips on your handgun is to <u>feel</u> them. Close your eyes and carefully concentrate on the sensation to feel the pressure on your hand from all sides of the handgun's grip. You want even pressure on all parts of your hand, especially the palm.

grips? If the factory grips are slippery, rub them down with wax. Use either surf board wax or canning wax to increase static friction. Result: You'll be able to hold on to the weapon better. Our editor, Andrew Gribble, who is a great handgunner in his own right, says this, "Another quick fix for either small or slippery grips is a garden glove with sticky rubber spots. Cut the fingers off."

Rubber grips have a disadvantage. They slow down a fast draw. You can live with a slower presentation however, if you know: "Action beats reaction." Unconventional methods of presentation always give

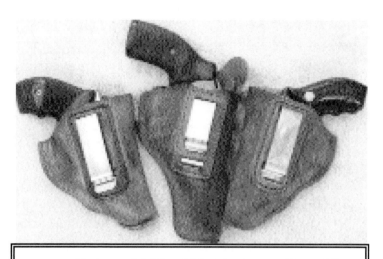

Early model Bianchi holsters are still providing good service on both these left and right handed belt rigs. What to notice, however, is the sticky rubber grips at left and center. While the grips work great in your hand, they catch on clothing and advertise your undercover status.

you an advantage over someone who draws from a holster. If you get into a dangerous situation, it's best to have your weapon out, concealed in a towel etc., and cocked and locked. We teach women in CONQUER CRIME: Danger? Take your pepper spray out. Carry it in plain sight and point it at any suspect. In a dangerous situation, your weapon needs to be ready to fire, even though not in plain sight.

WHERE YOUR FINGER CREATES DIRECTION

The trigger on your handgun is a critical part. You want the release to be sudden—-crisp. The pull has to be light—-about four pounds. To make all that happen, you need a gunsmith.

Consider your trigger finger, which must come straight to the rear rather than off to either side. National Match Pistol Team gunsmith Daniel Norwood said, "wider triggers with serrations give the shooter

> Three kinds of triggers found on various handguns. Flat serrations on left give you the most feel.

TRIGGER SURFACES

Serrated   Flat   Oval

more sensation on his finger." That's for target shooting, and Dan would know; he built two national match winners. As real live combat shooters know, however, wide triggers catch on holsters and are unsuitable for combat. Also, screw-on trigger shoes can come loose just at the wrong time.

While at the gunsmith's, some gun writers recommend bevel cuts on the chamber mouths of your revolver so your speed loader drops in slightly misaligned rounds easier. No sale! Those bevels don't allow the chamber to support a fired cartridge where it needs it most---in the high pressure area. If you want your speed loader to be quicker, use a pointed round nose or semi-wadcutter round.

Automatics are becoming quite popular and you can do a lot to improve them. First, have a gunsmith bevel the opening of the magazine well or add on a beveled-mouth extension. I want you to be able to jam a new mag in without looking and have the bevels guide it right in there. Install felt or rubber pads on the bottom of your magazines, too. That way you won't slow down due to pain on your palm and the mags won't dent when they hit concrete.

One thing more your gunsmith ought to do might help your auto pistol and this is important: Have him "throat" the ramp. You do this if your auto is touchy about feeding certain bullet types from the magazine into the chamber. Once a gunsmith polishes and bevels the ramp, your auto should accept all kinds of rounds, including wadcutters.

HANDGUN SIGHTING SYSTEMS

If you use conventional sights, this is the criterion: You must be able to see the front sight of the weapon clearly with your arm extended. If the blade appears to be fuzzy, buy prescription shooting glasses. The most basic requirement in shooting handguns is to align sights and you will never achieve that if your front sight is out of focus.

NIGHT SHOOTING

All handguns come with sights for daytime shooting, but most of the vermin in our society operate at night. Because of that, you need to install some kind of night shooting device. If you want to hit a target under poor light conditions, you need a highly visible front sight. This holds true for deliberate sight alignment or fast point shooting in darkness.

Through the years, the gun industry has tried everything---paint in all kinds of colors, plastic inserts, ivory and gold lines horizontal and vertical, and beads of all shapes. Today we have scopes, lasers, dots, and tritium. Under the right conditions, most of these do the job well. The cheapest, however, is the gold or brass half round bead installed on the ramp of your front blade. You can make one, and either you or a gunsmith can install it. It's sturdy, effective, and long-lasting.

BUILDING THE GOLD BEAD SIGHT

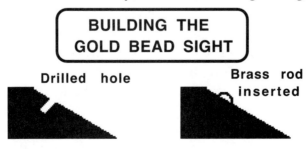

Drilled hole   Brass rod inserted

From your local hardware store, purchase a round brass rod. Shape one end with a fine file so it's a polished half sphere. Drill a hole into your front ramp to accept a small piece of rod(about 1/8th inch deep). Don't give up your pistol's day job. Make sure the hole you drill begins far enough down from the top of the ramp so that with bead installed, you can still see your (square) day sights. With blue loctite and a soft faced hammer, drive the brass rod into the hole. Polish with brass cleaner and spray it with lacquer so it stays shiny. Now, you're ready for night intruders.

Laser sights have increased in popularity. If the gun goes off and surprises you while the laser red dot is on target, there will be a hole where the red dot used to be. However, Dave doesn't recommend them for police work. Lots of parts means lots of things can go wrong. Do not drop one. Target acquisition is often slow while you're trying to search for the red dot. Also, the minute you flip the switch, you go into showbiz and announce your position. Finally, you put your life in the hands of batteries that may have been laying around with your gun in storage for who knows how long.

At a recent SHOT show, I tried several of these sights out. Midway between hip and eye level, I pointed at a reflector place over a hundred feet away and got right on. Lasers can be invaluable for training. Shine one against our wobble grid. They provide the most precise method of telling you what your wobble is from various shooting positions. It tells you about various holds including Isosceles, Weaver, or my own PAUL hold. Of course, the position which causes the least wobble is the most stable--and that's the position you need to drop into for a long range shot.

During a real shooting event, you would think lasers might compel you to squeeze the trigger while the red dot remains on target. Most often, the opposite is true. When the shooter sees the dot on target, he jerks the trigger, thus causing the dot <u>and the bullet</u> to move off target just as the gun fires. As with fixed iron sights, if the gun doesn't go off as a <u>surprise</u>, you probably disturbed sight alignment with the trigger jerk.

You can also buy scope sights with a dot reticule. As soon as the reticule is on the target, you let one fly. That's fine for hunting, but for street work the scope adds weight and bulk which is difficult and unwieldy. Other sight systems are more practical. Scopes work best on long barreled, high-powered handguns. Perhaps the best sights are fixed. Drift punch the rear sight and set it. Once set, it won't move. Adjustable sights have a way of losing zero when least expected.

CLEANING

Methods for cleaning vary, and a lot of information exists on the subject. Basically, you need to keep all the moving parts of any weapon clean and lubed. You also <u>must</u> clean the bore! Any copper or lead fouling you leave in there will eventually cause flyers---shots that go nowhere near the rest of your group. Bore cleaning is a tedious and repetitious job. Fire-lapping makes a mirror-smooth inside, so cleaning doesn't take as long and you won't experience as much fouling.

SECURITY

With the proliferation of weapons in this country, many children discover and play with parents' guns. Those kids often shoot themselves and friends. Therefore many states have now passed a law making parents responsible for not securing their weapons. In addition to the law, it makes good sense to secure your handgun. At the same time, remove all the signs on your car and home which relate to firearms—-they're number one burglar lures (see CONQUER CRIME).

You can now buy a mini-safe with four push buttons to which only you know the sequence. Trigger locks are better than nothing. One cheap way to secure a revolver is to open the cylinder and use a bicycle lock secured to a "U" bolt set in concrete.

Many handguns offered for sale can use help. Improve the grip, fix up the sights, make it night-shootable, and keep it clean. Then, you and your handgun can go the distance.

> When Dave worked motorcycle enforcement, he used a lanyard. He writes, "I like to tie a string on anything I can't afford to lose." Lanyards are cheap insurance. We're for gun control. Push forward gently against the tie while shooting so you hit what you aim at.

Chapter 8

METHODS OF CARRY

When you carry your handgun in a holster, we call that the conventional way because it leads to conventional presentation. You draw your weapon. Everybody can see what you are doing. If you're fast, they barely see it happen. Many handgunners don't practice enough, however. That's half fast.

Because we know that, we teach unconventional methods of carrying your handgun. Methods of gun-carry parallel the methods of knife-carry you will find in my book, EVERYBODY'S KNIFE BIBLE.

> Dave---writing as Confucius:
>   "One gun in hand worth two in holster."

A FINE GUN BOOK
Great way to carry a gun. Bigger the gun, the bigger the book you'll need. Leave some of the pages at the beginning and end of the book so you can lay it on a table open and be ready to draw by flipping the pages. Even better, shoot straight ahead out through the side of the book.

I suppose the cheapest way to carry a handgun is in a brown paper bag. That's not so bad either. Most would think you were concealing a bottle, but with the slightest hole in the side of the bag, your trigger finger could easily cause the weapon to discharge through the paper. Tool bags, book bags, or backpacks do the same. In CONQUER CRIME, How to Be Your Own Bodyguard, I wrote about a good way to carry a gun on the beach. It's a hand towel sewed to make a pocket in a beach towel of the same material and color. Handguns fit in all kinds of boxes, including a tupperware container under the seat of your car. You can attach parachute cord to most of these carriers so that a pull on the line puts the weapon at your disposal. Attach (glue, velcro) the parachute cord to a place on the floor underneath the brake pedal.

The idea of an unconventional presentation is this: You get your hand on the weapon long before the trouble starts. That is the best idea for women. Walking back to underground parking, for example, having a hand on a weapon in your purse makes sure you can just about outdraw anyone. Why? You don't have to draw. Shoot through the bag. Pockets in your shirt, coat, or pants also provide an unconventional carry. If you choose this way to go, use a hammerless weapon or a bobbed hammer spur. Jacket pocket carries will show less outline if you use a jacket pocket holster. Another benefit is this: They help keep the weapon in one position. Incidentally, if you carry that way, **nothing** else goes in that pocket. Keys and coins can be a tremendous bother if you need to fire quickly. Also, without a pocket holster, consider using a piece of velcro on the weapon so it attaches to the jacket pocket. It will keep the weapon in place so your hand can locate it quickly.

A popular unconventional method is the waist band carry, which works best with 4+ inch barrels. Waist band holsters help to keep the weapon secure. Note that if you carry this way, you may be at risk in the restroom. The gun falls out on the floor. Your posterior needs <u>only one</u> hole; secure your weapon prior to lowering pants.

CONVENTIONAL METHODS OF CARRYING

Since most people carry a handgun in a holster, we need to tell you this: Your holster must provide these features. Also, you need more than one holster for each weapon because of the various ways in which you dress.

1. Avoid holsters with flaps to keep rain, mud, and leaves away from your gun. For city work, it has to allow for quick and easy presentation. The quicker you can draw, the more time you have to aim.

2. The holster should be designed to aid you---not only in drawing quickly, but in pointing the gun in the general direction in which lead placement is required. It

should also provide you with a solid index (shooting grip) quickly. You don't want to be trying to get a grip during a fast draw.

3. A firm (not bouncing around) carry. Mold the holster to the weapon.

4. The weapon must be where you always know it is, even after a hard physical fight. Anchor the holster to one part of your body firmly.

5. Remember, you need to conceal your weapon. A holster that makes it stick out through your jacket will cause someone else to be on guard and perhaps draw first.

6. The holster needs to be light weight; the weapon by itself will be heavy enough.

7. Comfort counts. You'll need to concentrate on several things while carrying, and discomfort will always interfere with your productivity while placing new holes in a target.

Dave's personal double shoulder holster rig. In order for one gun to back up the other, it's best if they both shoot the same kind of ammunition. This rig provided Dave with both security and utility. That's for combat. Hunters and survivors are better served by two different calibers.

8. Holsters provide security from theft. Weapons are wonderful things that "lengthen & strengthen" our sphere of defense. Lose your weapon to the other side, however, and his sphere of defense is lengthened & strengthened. So you absolutely do not want to lose your weapon. Holsters

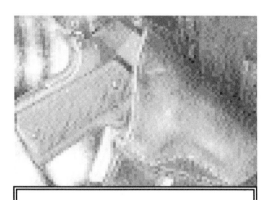

Hip holster for the Colt Officer's Model Colt .45 ACP. Note the way Dave carries this SAO---cocked and locked.

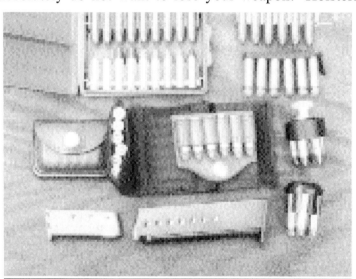

If you carry a gun, you have to carry ammo as well. A variety of pouches and speed loaders are available. Attach bullet hoops to seat belts in your vehicle or the outside of your backpack for easy reaching.

that might put your weapon at risk of loss would be paddles for the small of the back, especially if you are a white male with a flat posterior. Holsters that give you more security against gun loss have spring retainers and snaps. For extra security, high rider holsters position your gun so you can clamp down on the butt with your elbow, i.e, a high rider.

9. If you carry a gun much, then you probably get into fist fights, chase people on foot at a full run or ride a horse. Good chance you will need your handgun. Make sure your method of carry secures your firepower until <u>you</u> remove it! Tie it to your body with a lanyard.

While this book takes a military outlook on engagements, tactical situations, etc, those factors don't normally come into play. Why? We live in a civilian world. Even though 65 people every day die from violence in the United States, many don't go around carrying a gun. Only 31 of our states issue permits to carry concealed. Even law enforcement officers don't use a gun often. So when confronted, it will probably be by surprise. That means your presentation will have to be quick and easy.

To decide on a location for handgun storage on your body, consider the following: Where do I want to carry this thing so it's least obvious, carries easily, adapts to my life style, is secure, but above all, makes presentation a snap? Do you play a sport that keeps certain muscles in top shape? If so, use those muscles for presentation. A good example would be archery, which keeps your deltoid tuned. For such a person, cross draw would be a well-supported-by-muscle-strength move. You'll note of course, that cross draw holsters provide more security. A grab from behind you would be awkward and you can defend an attempt from the front.

Shoulder holsters under suit coats come in a variety of styles. Adjust the straps so the holster carries the

Shoulder holsters carry long barrels up and out of the way---securely. Most shooters don't do this, but often straps on shoulder holsters can carry extra magazines, knives, etc. to keep you well equipped. Use glue or velcro to attach them. Why not add an extra magazine holder on your shoulder holster harness? Test the orientation of the magazine. You want to reach for it with your non-shooting hand and have it ready to fit into the gun butt without having to finger it around and perhaps drop it. You need to grab it---one grip, one move, one jam---into the magazine well.

weapon comfortably, then mark the straps so the adjustment will always be the same. No matter what kind of holster you decide on, make sure it doesn't move around on your body. I want it to be within a quarter inch of its proper place always. That way, when you need it, it's there.

A small back-up in a Bianchi holster may save your life. Dave says: <u>"I would rather have it and not need it than to need it and not have it."</u> Words we can <u>live</u> by.

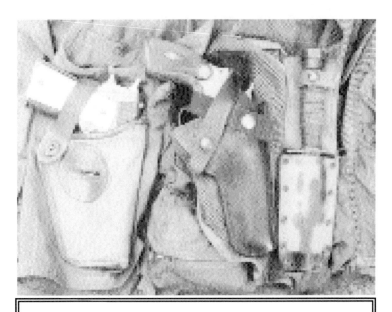

G.I. surplus survival vests make handy holsters with pockets and room for anything. Most Army/Navy surplus stores carry all kinds of tactical web gear. Use an awl to sew on any holster you need.

Carry a not-so-obvious---and therefore holstered---back-up. The holster for that will have to keep your gun secure, give you quick access, and hopefully keep that second gun undiscovered. Cordura holsters respond to sweat and water a lot better than leather. But leather holsters are well known for speed.

Once you decide on a method of carry, stick with it. Changing methods of carry is not a good idea. Under stress, you need to draw from one location without trying to remember which holster you are wearing. Carrying a gun around is an inconvenience. The method you choose to carry makes it less troublesome and more available.

> Handgun shooting competitions have given rise to shooting methods that simply **will not work** in most practical shooting circumstances. Even with a good gun and special ammunition, many shooters simply can't hit a target during the pressure of combat.

CHAPTER 9

HANDGUN USE

In THE RIFLE RULES of this set we emphasized the importance of good ammunition and an improved gun for creating super accuracy. With handguns, shooting proficiency is mostly up to the shooter. When Path Finder published *EVERYBODY'S OUTDOOR SURVIVAL GUIDE,* we hired Army Green Beret Silver Star winner and black belt judo expert Rick Woodcroft to write on several subjects. In his chapter on hand to hand combat, he quotes Confederate General Jubal Early, who said "Get there fustus with the mostest." Handgunners need to learn that.

SHOOTING TIMES HAVE CHANGED

Shooting a handgun used to be a stand-up, day time sport. The handgunner would turn sideways to the target, extend his or her arm, line up the sights and fire deliberately and slowly. Every shooting factor was measured and controlled---time, amount and kind of ammo, target movement (none) and shooting distance. You had plenty of time to BRASS—-relax, breathe, aim and squeeze. The winner of a match was the person who could punch more holes in the center of a stationary bullseye.

Handgun shooting has something in common with sports today--you have to practice like you play. Handguns are designed to be shot during the day; most criminal conflicts occur at night. You'll be amazed at the difference.

Most writers will tell you that a handgun will defend you only at distances up to 50 yards. That's too simple. I taught one woman in Germany to shoot a .45 auto and within ten minutes she had scored on a 55 gallon drum barrel 100 yards away. Of course, the bullet only dented it. Most handgun bullets won't penetrate at a long distance.

To determine the effectiveness of any handgun at long range, ask two questions: A. Can you place the bullet on target that far out? B. Will the projectile have any stopping power after slowing down way out there? Thus, if you shoot a .38 Special with wadcutters, a distant target one hundred yards away won't be hurt too badly. If you increase the powder load and use a lighter bullet that will expand in the target, you'll get results.

What about A? Can you shoot? Small aiming on short sight bases create huge misses at long distance. Suppose, for example, that your barrel length is only two inches and you mis-align your sights by 1/64th of an inch. At 50 yards, that's a twelve inch miss. For long distance, you need a long sight base.

OTHER FACTORS

In addition to barrel length, how well can you shoot? Is your wobble small, or does it look like you're training to be a flag waver? Does your trigger finger have a Ph.D. or does it wiggle like a kindergarten kid trying to pick his nose? How's your vision? Are your sights highly visible? Shine on the front blade of handguns from holster wear makes good sight alignment impossible. See your gunsmith or darken your sights with a candle. For night firing, install dots.

If you're not hitting, find out why. First, use our wobble grid to tell you how steady you are and whether your trigger pressure during the snap is pushing off to one side. Convert your wobble to bullet placement error at a specific distance. Remember, one MOA equals 1/2 inch at 50 yards and 1/4 inch at 25 yards. A 40 minute wobble causes 10" groups at 25 yards.

After learning your wobble from various positions, train. Imitate real shooting conditions as best you can, set up targets, and find out what you and your handgun can do together. Buy some 8" paper plates and hang them at various distances away. As you increase your shooting distance by shooting groups too large to be effective, make a mental note of your shooting distance limitation. Then, don't shoot at longer distances. You may only wound game. In combat, you'll fail to hit, perhaps hit something else, and worst of all, advertise your position to attract incoming lead.

SHOOTING FOR REAL OCCURS AT NIGHT

At night the muzzle flash of the weapon may not blind you, but you will think you've gone blind because your eye's iris will contract due to muzzle flash light. If you shoot a handgun with both eyes open, change now. Close your weak eye hard before firing. You need one saved eye to see what's going on. Your target may be moving, especially after a close round or one that came through his defense barricade. If you stand still during practice, you'll do the same during combat. That won't work, you need to shoot and move. You will probably shake from the adrenaline in your bloodstream.

New methods of holding have now enabled law enforcement officers to shoot better and faster. Notably, the two handed Weaver hold gave the handgunner quicker multi-target shooting mobility and kept his sights decently aligned. Note that it relies on muscle tension to hold the weapon. At short distance, who cares? At longer distances, however, muscle tension causes extra wobble so it's more difficult to hold on target. Other shooters opted for the isosceles hold—-both hands on the weapon straight out in front—-and turn the torso left and right to face each target. My own PAUL system: Platform Accuracy, Unitized <u>Level</u>, locks up the weapon and permits the shooter to fire from the hip with a level barrel. Level barrel is good---if your target happens to be on the same level you are. For shooting up or downhill, you're much better off with instinctive point shooting.

CREATE STRESS DURING PRACTICE

Don't practice leisurely to prepare yourself for combat. Shooting confrontations begin and end in a quick flash of time. You don't have time to think. Brass flies, bullets crack past you and ricochets fly everywhere. Try to approximate the strain of combat. At least train under the stress of strong physical exertion. Run up a hill in the dark before shooting so your heart's pumping as if it had just received a shot of adrenaline. Competition with trophies and prizes often make shooters nervous. Good. Train with a partner. At night, one partner can cue the other by setting off firecrackers, throwing tin cans ahead of the shooter from behind, etc. Practice stalking approaches as a team. Learn sounds each partner makes to communicate. We want NO friendly fire incidents.

Dry firing is an important part of every shooter's training. It consists of hundreds of trigger squeezes with the sights lined up against a blank wall (white) to make sure the sights don't move when the trigger snaps. Even better, dry fire while aiming at our wobble grid so you can measure the slightest deviation. When you shoot live, it should be at a target with scoring rings, under the pressure of time, and in competition with other shooters. Smoke, noise, recoil and flying hot brass all help approximate the stress of the real thing.

THEORY OF RELATIVE TARGET SIZE

Imagine yourself in a shooting contest. From the firing line, other shooters fire at a 12" bullseye, but your bullseye is half that size. With that disadvantage, you might lose. In combat shooting I want your opponent to have a disadvantage like that. The idea when you shoot any weapon is to hit. That's the opposite of miss, which is what you want your opponent to do. Out in the open, reduce your body size to less than 50% so you double his chances of missing. You need to practice this. Draw, crouch, fire. Even better, draw, sit, and fire.

> Law enforcement guys need to design a competition in which shooters get add-on points for shrinking into a smaller target when shooting.

From behind a barricade, you reduce your target body exposure even more. Don't run in a straight line, zig-zag. Few handgun shooters can hit a moving target.

Of course, shoot back. Eliminate all of the causes of misses. To find out what causes a miss, ask, "*What could go wrong when I pull this trigger.*" You'll be amazed at all the answers. Some are:

Sights are mis-aligned; the front blade is either too high, low, or off to one side.

Sights couldn't be aligned because it was night and nothing was added to make the sights visible in the dark.

Shooter couldn't align sights because the shooter was out of breath, or adrenaline caused shooter to develop shakes. Even more common, shooter had sights aligned but failed to get a good sight picture because he aimed at the whole target body rather than focusing on one small part of it, such as a belt buckle or nose. Dave's favorite quote from the movie "The Patriot": "Remember, aim at little, miss a little."

Sights <u>were</u> aligned, but trigger jerk or a press too hard from the heel of the shooter's hand on the pistol butt pulled them off so they were mis-aligned (high) when the bullet flew. A common error when shooting from the hip.

Sights were aligned---on target---with good trigger squeeze---but with no follow through and the wrist flopped or the barrel moved.

I'm sure you get the idea. Sight misalignment makes bullets miss. Listen to this truth. I was a member of a high level Army Marksmanship Detachment and I heard this in the lectures to the troops over and over again: To shoot well, you have to **align your sights,** and then cause the hammer to fall **without disturbing your sight alignment.** It sounds simple, doesn't it? But it's more difficult than counting beans in a jar while someone is giving you phone numbers to memorize. That's why the three great western virtues in America were: To ride, tell the truth, and shoot straight. Our forefathers, full of Godly wisdom, knew what kind of self control and concentration good shooting required.

TO SHOOT STRAIGHT

Eliminate <u>all</u> the causes of shooting crooked! Once lined up, your sights indicate the barrel (bullet delivery tube) is in line with the target. Now, squeeze the trigger so you don't make your barrel (sights) point somewhere else just before the bullet fires. <u>The number one cause of missed shots is jerking the trigger, even if ever so slightly.</u> Could a jerk occur if you aimed more carefully? Certainly. You may have <u>had</u> it perfect, but you destroyed it.

To be an all around good pistol shot (various ranges, up and down, different stances), learn to shoot instinctively. Don't be deliberate in using the pistol's sights. Point the pistol at your target, concentrate on <u>one small part</u> of that target, and squeeze. This is done in one fluid motion, slowly at first, faster as you improve.

GOOD FUNDAMENTALS ARE CRITICAL

Even before you arrive at a skill level that enables you to shoot fast, you have several basics to learn. Follow this progressive outline.

1. Trigger control is a must. During dry firing, do not aim at a <u>target</u>. Otherwise you'll learn to jerk just as the sights wobble past the bullseye, which is exactly the opposite of the skill you're trying to acquire. Lift weights, do pushups, jog, or whatever. As your muscles improve, your wobble will diminish. In the meantime, <u>trust it.</u> Smooth squeezers sometimes become trigger jerkers because they try to make the hammer drop just as sight picture is perfect.

Simply stare at the sights, with your focus on the front blade. Squeeze. When the hammer drops, note any change in sight alignment. When your sights stay perfectly still after many hammer drops, your trigger finger is passing the test. You've learned to maintain sight alignment.

Now, darken the room. Use the same dry fire technique while using sights which have been modified for night shooting.

Make sure your trigger control causes the hammer to drop as a surprise. Trust your wobble. With a good sight alignment, even a huge wobble will allow you to hit a target far out, but misaligned sights cause horrific misses. The slightest disturbance is often enough to create disaster. Since jerking occurs more frequently with large caliber pistols, learn to shoot with a .22.

With negligible low caliber recoil, you can concentrate on the straight-to-the-rear squeeze while sight alignment never varies.

2. To hit your target, hold the pistol with perfect sight alignment. Ignoring wobble, begin to put pressure on the trigger. Maintain 100% mental attention on your front sight with the <u>unfocused</u> target in the background. Concentrate **only** on your front sight as your finger increases pressure on the trigger. The hammer <u>must drop as a surprise</u>. The end result will be: You will hit your target---somewhere in the area of your wobble.

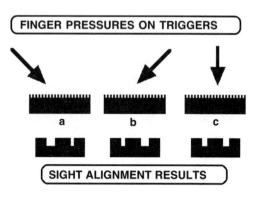

3. When you can fire single action and cause the hammer to drop without disturbing sight alignment, you're ready to learn the same skill in the double action mode. It requires a different index (hold on the handgun), because you need more strength to bring the trigger to the rear and lift the hammer at the same time. As before, stare at your front sight and learn to cause the hammer to drop without disturbing sight alignment. It takes practice.

4. At a live firing range, start with a .22 or use <u>light</u> loads in a .38 Special. Too heavy a caliber in the beginning may cause a shooter to flinch or start jerking triggers.

5. As soon as you can shoot light loads with consistently good scores, buy or build rounds with

heavier bullets. The same controlled trigger squeeze, sight alignment, sight picture and surprise method applies. Be careful; when long distance is the next best thing to being there, sight alignment and trigger squeeze insure success.

Now you have learned to shoot in a <u>controlled environment</u>. You know the distance, you know the load, the time was adequate and always the same, and you shot in daylight.

However, handgun shooting for real most often occurs in an <u>uncontrolled environment</u>! The perp or burglar comes in on you at 0400 from a place from which you didn't even suspect he'd be. You don't get to shoot on level ground. There may be broken glass on the floor. He's shooting at you. You don't know the range. Therefore, once you learn the basics, it's time to diversify practice.

Learn to shoot instinctively. It's easy to point at anything with your upper forearm bone (radius). If you index (grip gun correctly), the barrel will be in line with your forearm. Once you can hit this way in daylight, you can do the same in darkness. Drop to a sitting or kneeling position and fire at sounds. Any method you use to shoot well without using your eyes makes you a good combat handgunner night and day.

ONE HAND SHOOTING FROM HIP

With only one hand in a quick draw, combat practice should include hip shooting out to 6 feet. With one hand extended, draw and shoot from 6 to 15 feet. At first, just make a smooth motion, out of your holster, point at the target and fire. "Point" means make sure to get the correct grip on your handgun when you draw the weapon and use the top of your arm to direct the barrel (in line with your forearm) at your target as you shoot. Practice one handed shooting from both left and right hands. You have to shoot around barricades from both sides.

At 15 to 25 feet draw and shoot with either a one or two-hand hold. See the Platform-Accuracy, Unitized-Level system he explained in *EVERYBODY'S OUTDOOR SURVIVAL GUIDE*. Two-hand holds become rigid when you lock your weapon into tension and compression with that slight shoulder rotation towards the shooting hand. Practice accurate two-handed shooting using your sights from 25 feet and further. Sight picture and trigger control become more important with long distance shooting.

DETERMINE HITTING DISTANCE FROM WOBBLE

No pistol shooter on any law enforcement department should work in the field without measuring wobble. This bears repeating: Wobble is always equal to a measurable cone of fire at any given distance. If you exceed that distance, your expanded cone of fire will probably create a miss. Measure periodically. As you improve, your wobble will decrease so your insured shooting distance will increase. Also, trigger disturbances will become less disruptive.

<u>Handgun combat</u> shooting requires a variety of skills. Learn them one at a time, then combine them to become a great combat handgunner. Each skill has specific definitions.

<u>Shooting position</u>. It can be prone, sitting, kneeling or any standing position. Learn to shoot from behind a barricade, rock, or tree.

<u>Presentation</u>. This word defines the act of removing your handgun from its storage place and bringing it to bear on target.

<u>Unconventional</u> presentations are made in such a way that nobody sees your gun. How about a weapon in a paper bag taped to a square plastic juice container? It looks like you are drinking something. The same goes for under the coat, hanging over your

arm, in a canvas tool bag, in a cut out book, or under a newspaper. These kinds of presentation are often best because you're ready to shoot without the short delay it takes to draw. Also, there is no tip-off to your enemy, and you don't have to disturb the crowd around you by flashing a gun. All you have to do is watch your opponent's hands; if the trouble escalates, your trigger pull is all it takes.

<u>Index</u>. Defines the way in which you grip the handgun. Correct indexing requires your barrel to be in line with your forearm. To maintain that index while firing, your hand should exert even pressure on all sides of the handgun grip. If someone smeared Vaseline all over your .44 magnum handgun's grip just before you fired it, you'd lose your index. Do the opposite. Grab your (improved) handgun grip properly.

<u>Target acquisition.</u> In all precision shooting, you must first align your sights, then cause those aligned sights to point at your target. Let's be careful to define "target." It's not the whole animal. It is not a door. It's a small visible part of your target, such as a belt buckle or door knob. That's what you aim at. Why? Because shooters miss when they don't focus on a small part, but merely aim in the general direction of the whole.

Once you've acquired a specific part of your target, cause the weapon to fire <u>without disturbing those sights</u>. That's why trigger control is so important. Under pressure, you have to bring the trigger straight to the rear. If you can't do that, why bother aligning the sights in the first place?

<u>Bullet delivery follow through.</u> It ain't over 'till it's over. Many a shooter makes this mistake under pressure. They align the sights, create a sight picture (on target) squeeze to the rear, and abandon the whole procedure as soon as the gun fires. Perhaps the wrist

flops, the arm moves, the grip (index) loosens up. Any or all of these can create a slight barrel movement and divert the bullet. This is best: Fire and "hold that thought" for a second after the gun goes off. As you hold the weapon steady with constant muscle pressure and an unchanging grip, think about directing the flight of the bullet with the muzzle of the gun--right to the small point on the target at which you aimed.

Shooting from the standing position with any weapon is the most unstable. Worse than that, when standing, you expose your <u>whole</u> body. On one knee, you're half that size. It takes about the same amount of time for the average shooter to drop to one knee and fire as it does to draw and fire while standing. The average bad guy on the street can't get a round off before you drop down if you shoot at the same time you are dropping down. Also, most first shots are high anyway because it's common to hold the muzzle up when shooting from the hip.

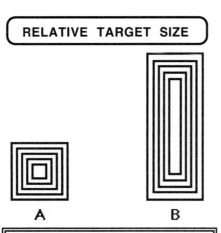

RELATIVE TARGET SIZE

A   B

The smaller you make yourself, the harder you are to hit. Look at B. Twice as easy. Proof that "stand-up" is for comedy; not handgun battle.

In the sitting position, you're a smaller target than when kneeling. While you draw, cross your ankles and sit as you send your lead flying. If you lay prone (with decent head cover), you have reduced your body target size to less than 15%. Most shooters simply can't hit a target that size from 25 yards away. Of course, if you're behind a barricade, only a portion of head and gun arm is exposed.

New positions to reduce relative size often provide the additional benefit of steadying your weapon. You become hard to hit while increasing your chances of hitting. One big advantage to using a wobble grid is finding out what shooting positions produce the least wobble. It's critical information, because sooner or later, you will have to take a long, meaningful shot with a handgun. Kneeling with a two-handed hold while resting against a barricade might be best for producing a steady (no-wobble) way to shoot. It's not the same for everyone, however. Therefore, work out dry firing on our wobble grid from a variety of positions until you find what's best.

COVER

Just about anything you get behind will slow down an incoming round. Bullets flying towards you need enough velocity to penetrate with enough bullet energy to cause the bullet to expand. <u>Anything</u> through which they pass before they hit you will slow the round down enough to save your life. Just as a small single engine pilot should look for places to land in an emergency, you should look for cover in any situation that could be dangerous. Pick the best cover you can find. Don't get over confident because you hide behind glass, a house wall, or a hollow core door. If the

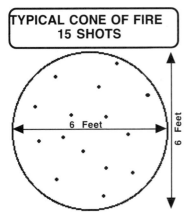

4.8 DEGREES OF BARREL AND TRIGGER SQUEEZE DEVIATION

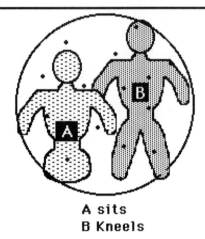

A sits
B Kneels

> Here's what it all means: You can shoot while you pop into a smaller stance. Once you get into that stance, you reduce your chances of taking an incoming round. How much? By the same percentage as your personal reduction in target size.

bullet looking for you came out of a .357 cartridge and is designed to penetrate, you'll even be at risk behind some trees.

Once you get behind cover, however, learn to use that stationary object as a rest for your pistol. Practice that way. On a close-in target, you wouldn't bother with a rest, but the Lord has blessed you if you get into a hot lead exchange at a far distance and a tree is convenient. With a steadied weapon and almost all of your shrunken body protected, you'll increase your chances of survival many fold.

PRESENTATION

Most of the time, your weapon tags along with you in a convenient device called a holster. Many shooting conflicts arise by surprise, so learning to draw and shoot is important. Even so, I don't like the conventional concept.

The best presentation is something like Bruce Lee's "Way of fighting without fighting." My version is, "Way of presentation without presentation". When you smell trouble, your weapon needs to be in your hand long before the conflict escalates and defines itself as deadly. With a secret handgun presentation already made, you can shoot first as soon as you see your life is in danger. Nobody sees the gun because it's disguised. The idea is to be ready long before serious trouble really starts, but not to cause any of that serious trouble by displaying your weapon.

INDEX

Some manuals ignore the importance of indexing. Here's a couple of important pistol pointers:

A. The barrel needs to be in line with your forearm, which lines up instinctively when you point at anything. You may be high or low, but your left/right alignment will be correct. Also, recoil must push straight on your forearm, otherwise the crooked side jolt will cause grip loss and your barrel will point somewhere else for your second shot.

The probability of losing your index after one shot increases if the material in your grips is somewhat slippery. That's one reason I have never been a fan of walnut checkered stocks. Canning or surfboard wax will improve your grip, much the same as the wax gives you traction on your surfboard. Also, wet or dry sandpaper wrapped around the stock under the grips will provide a better grip on the front and back of the gun butt.

TARGET ACQUISITION

Acquire your target. Again I'm bothered because all the manuals and books teach you to do this by sight. In many cases, you do it by sound. In the movie, *BODYGUARD*, Kevin Costner chases an assassin in the snow. He falls to his knees and closes his eyes. Why? On both knees, he reduced his personal target area by more than half. With eyes closed, he could concentrate on listening. The plan: Let both ears line up on the sound so that your nose is pointing in the direction of the footsteps. Then point the weapon out level in line with your nose and squeeze—-a lot. Theory: A close round scares him into a move, and quick follow-up round will find him. Practice this way. It will help you to shoot accurately in pitch black. Your ears hear, your nose points at the sound and with a strict isosceles (triangle) hold with the barrel level--let lead fly!

Meanwhile, back to target acquisition by sight. All factory handgun sights (narrow rear notch) require you to bring your weapon up to eye level and search for the front blade with just a little space on each side. It's a slow process. To pick up a little speed widen your rear

FASTER SIGHT ALIGNMENT WITH WIDER NOTCH

Note misalignment error or B

A   **B**

Note the misalignment on B. We drew it that way to teach you: Wide notches in rear sights lead to left/right error. See extra space on right? However, they make it much easier and quicker to find your front blade.

sight notch (ceramic triangular file). Then re-blue so you don't create a sun reflection off the shiny surface. In addition add a gold bead or white dot to your front blade for higher visibility at night.

Close in, don't worry about bringing your weapon up anywhere near your eyes; it takes too long. Sights are for distances over 25 feet from behind cover. Maybe a car, a dumpster or a brick wall can stop a bullet for you. When you rest your weapon up against a barricade to steady it, your sights will be more effective.

Don likes it if on the way up to your line of sight, you let a round or two fly. It's best when those rounds hit the ground in front of the perp, bounce up and take

> To be more sure of hitting your target, focus on a small part of the target area. Concentrate on a small spot on the big target and let your hand/eye coordination surprise you. Misses aimed at that tiny area will still hit the larger target.

asphalt with them. Dave doesn't do that. He regards ammunition as a precious commodity and he doesn't care for ricochet rounds. Also, he wants your focus to be intent on hitting one small part of the target, nothing else. No co-authors agree on everything; we just present both sides. Figure out which way works best for you.

Never count on one scoring hit as sufficient. Once you've fired, keep on firing until you know for certain the threat has been eliminated. Be ready to hammer more rounds home; it's never over until it's really over.

HOW TO DEVELOP A SHOOTING PLAN

As you know, handguns finish third in range power and accuracy behind rifles, then shotguns. However,

> Here's the rule of combat shooting:
> **The closer your adversary is,
> the more speed you need.**

> Caution: Many a cop owns real property as a result of having tried to render first aid and save the life of someone he just shot. That property is a small piece of land---in a cemetery. Do not approach motionless targets if you can't see both hands. They will shoot you as a matter of principle.

most handgun confrontations are pistol vs. pistol. Develop your shooting plan around these vital elements:
1. Your presentation and target acquisition speed.
2. Range, the distance from you to the target.
3. How far you have to run in order to reach cover.
4. Ammo to waste? What's your basic load?
5. How long is your down time? Can you improve it?
6. Are you a solo act, or do you have a good shooting partner?
7. Develop a plan for both night and day.

YOUR SHOOTING PLAN EXPANDED

1. If you are as fast as G Gordon Liddy, and you can get a round on target quicker than most, put your effort into shooting. Remember: **Action beats reaction.** Be first! Second place sucks--like a chest wound.

2. Is he farther away than you can shoot accurately? From your MOA wobble results you know the distance at which you can place an accurate round. Take cover; perhaps let a round go while you <u>get moving</u>.

For a long shot in the field you'll be more accurate with a two-hand hold and a rest. For law enforcement officers, firearms superiority means more than staying alive. It means staying confident, an attitude bad guys read on the street.

3. If the distance to cover is too far away, you may have to shoot it out. Get your body target small and steady your weapon. If you can get one or two rounds off—-enough to suppress incoming fire while you

move—-go for the cover. A zig-zag running target will be almost impossible for him to hit, and as soon as you're secure, you can either call for help or swap lead with relative safety.

4. Consider your basic load. For day to day moving about, I only carry six rounds in a .45 Star PD. When Dave carries this gun, he always brings an extra mag. If I were working in law enforcement in a city, a stacked 9 mm magazine with two back-up mags would be more appropriate. I could provide fire suppression, disable vehicles etc, and know I had plenty of ammunition. Also, I could carry a better variety of rounds. Some of my ammo sizzles and some bullets are hard enough to penetrate elephant skin.

> During a fire fight in San Francisco, a perp walked up on a police officer while he was reloading and shot him in the back of the head.
> Tragedies like this occur because police officers don't get enough weapons training. Fifty rounds a month is almost minimal. LAPD recommends 80, but PD's don't have the money for ammunition. We have found a way to train that doesn't cost money. Wobble grid practice to determine maximum shooting and trigger control, use of cover, and gun handling. Finally, face off training with self size reduction.

5. If operating solo, watch your down time. This is the most dangerous time in your life. Get prepared. Speed loader ready, and perhaps change after four or five shots if you get a downtime chance. You can't afford to be empty for a long time; it's too risky, especially if against multiple targets. Increasingly, perpetrators are either counting shots or picking up on the silence and killing police officers during down time (See *CONQUER CRIME* and learn why you reload before you're empty). Work on improving your magazine reloading times.

6. In my book *GREAT LIVIN in GRUBBY TIMES,* I explained how two good team members working together are much better than three opponents. With a partner, practice shooting as a team. Some do that now, but they stand side-by-side and fire at the same time. That's wrong. Never let both guns empty at the same time. Make sure your down times (for reloading) are staggered. Note: Mix 'n match magazine loaders can use tracers on certain rounds, say # 9 in a stack of 14. That tells your partner exactly how close you are to empty so he can open steady fire about the time you reload. Next, learn to maneuver. Don't get into a gunfight where you're both in the same geographic position. We like it best when both partners are behind good cover, but one has flanked the enemy from the side.

One more important point: In the movies, one guy yells, "Cover me." and takes off running. Don't do that! Several disasters could occur. The message didn't get through. The covering partner was on round 12 of a 15 round mag. His gun jams. He himself delivers the same message and moves. Finally, many shooters expose more of their body when they shoot. So the partner gets hit while you're moving.

7. Available light is an important element in developing a shooting plan. Furthermore, if you only have limited time for practice, do it at night. Learn muzzle flash, movement in the dark with only one good (non-shooting) eye, and shooting at noise. Practice the way you'll play. Modify your weapon so you can see the line-up of your sights and barrel in the dark.

How are you dressed? If you wear a lot of glitz (on a uniform) it may be difficult to move without being discovered. When I worked as a San Diego cop, my leather squeaked and my badge shined. Remember— no matter day or night, always try to position yourself so you are in less light than your enemy. For defense shooters—-people who will be defending a home or acting as a security guard for others, put motion detector lights outside your house. Set night lights to shine on your intruder. You stay in the dark.

WHAT TO SHOOT AT?

Hit what's available. If you can see it, make it holey. Also, look at shadows and reflections and use your imagination. Learn to pick out targets as reflected off glass, car paint, and bumps in otherwise straight

> Criminals and gang people now know this light trick and use it a lot. Air rifles and sling shots knock out lights. That's a tip-off. If you enter an area in which street lights have been destroyed, be wary!

shadow lines. Movement will be a dead giveaway. As long as <u>you</u> are still and searching, the advantage is yours. If you know your target is hiding behind something you can punch through, try it with a round you put together for penetration. Caution: Rounds which penetrate barricades seldom stop there. Think, if you can, about what or who your bullet might ventilate a block away. Do not shoot a child!

Improve your view. Under cars you can see for a long distance while behind good cover. Drop down, level your barrel and put a round through your enemy's foot. Score? Put a second round in the same place; a body will soon be landing there.

Maneuver, but don't expose yourself. Perhaps climb to a higher place so you have a better field of fire. Sometimes a quick few steps to the side will provide better cover. Almost always move to the rear. This baloney about "never retreat" is some office puke's stab at manhood. BULL! If you retreat, you open the shooting range. Since you can shoot better bullets farther away with more precision, you'll win. Above all, YOU won't get shot. Nobody ever wins a war against crime by dying for his city.

Expand your thinking beyond sending lead directly to your target. A lot of times you can easily hit something else that will damage the enemy more than a bullet. Street lights overhead, for example, will shower broken glass down on the bad guy. Is he hiding under a vehicle? Give the car a new custom look by lowering it. Shoot the tires out. That should "settle" things. If downhill behind a barricade in a street, punch open the gas tanks in a few cars up above him to create a high octane river. Then send a full jacket round to the cement so things light up. If the surfaces in the area consist of concrete or rocks, use full jacketed round nose bullets to billiard-ball into his general area. If you cast bullets, use a high antimony blend and quench the round by dropping it into water straight out of the mold while hot. Re-cast wheel weights gathered from a tire shop bounce nicely. Pewter is even better.

TRIGGER CONTROL

Although most trigger jerks send a bullet into the lower left corner of a target, (right handed shooters) you just can't be sure where in tarnation your finger will make the barrel point when you jerk. Without controlling your trigger finger, learning target acquisition (sighting) doesn't make much sense; you're only going to push the barrel out of line just as the gun fires anyway.

Therefore, you need to exercise your trigger finger until every round you fire does nothing to disturb your sight alignment. The time honored way is by dry firing. But that doesn't mean just pick up a pistol and start pulling the trigger. No, you grip the weapon with the proper index and use a wobble reducing stance. Do not aim at a target. Doing that teaches you to "jerk" when the sight picture is perfect. Dry firing is best done against our wobble grid with a light (laser) and a coach. Literally stare at your front sight and see if it deflects at all as your hammer drops. Practice. To give your trigger finger a fine education, you can also use a light or laser sight attached to your weapon. Sight and dry fire on our wobble grid in a darkened room.

Basic trigger control is a **slow squeeze**, a gentle, firm and slow pressure-increase squeeze straight to the rear. This is the squeeze we use for single action shooting (auto or revolver with hammer cocked) at a non-moving target while (probably) shooting from a rest. Even though it's the easiest of trigger squeezes, it takes a while to learn. You need to get so good at it that it happens automatically. Always use the same spot on your finger, positioned in the same place on your trigger, and be careful to watch your sights as the hammer falls. If you can't do that while completely relaxed in your home, you won't be able to hit squat when shooting under stress.

After a **slow squeeze**, graduate to fast press. Increase pressure on the trigger quickly. Your finger already knows what it feels like to come straight to the rear, and you do that now---only faster. Don't break discipline. The **fast press** is nothing more than a slow squeeze which happens quickly. This

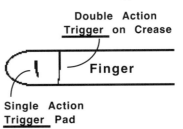

is the squeeze you generally employ for hip shooting at targets less than 7 yards away. To get good at this, practice on the rapid fire segment of competition, which is five rounds in 20 seconds and then five rounds in 10 seconds. That's the kind of practice you need.

Advanced trigger squeeze techniques enable you to shoot long distances with a double action accurately. To do this trick, teach your finger the **two-stage trigger squeeze**. The idea is to press the trigger and cause the hammer to come <u>almost</u> all the way to the rear. With your last finger joint wrapped around the trigger, you may feel the tip of your finger touch the trigger guard. Stop there. Check sight alignment, and then squeeze the last portion of the DA trigger pull to fire the weapon. Some fingers on some guns don't feel the trigger guard. Therefore, many shooters install a slight rubber extension on their pistol grips to use as a sensory spot. When the tip of the trigger finger comes in contact, the shooter knows just a little more pressure will fire the gun.

Two stage trigger squeezes will be most employed when the shooter is trying to put out a narrow cone of fire on a moving target. With only six rounds, some shooters feel at a disadvantage. But revolvers are safe and accurate; that's why many still use them to this day. Many revolver shooters working in the field are good shots. Why? Like single shot riflemen, revolver shooters often aim carefully because they know back-up rounds won't be immediately available. With a two stage trigger squeeze, they can be fast **and** accurate.

PRACTICE WITH LIGHT LOADS?

Yes. Practice with heavy loads, especially for novice shooters, often creates the tendency to flinch, jerk, and otherwise avoid recoil. Light loads, on the other hand, insure that good shooting habits develop in a new shooter. It doesn't matter that at some future time, during a gunfight, the added recoil will create a problem for the shooter. Dave speaks from combat experience when he says, "During a gunfight, you won't feel recoil or hear the blast. But practice with heavy loads makes you flinch and jerk the trigger so you develop bad habits. Therefore, your chances of missing your targets increase substantially.

NIGHT SHOOTING

As you know, most of your serious shooting will occur during darkness. When you can't see anything, it's best to take cover and tease the other guy into shooting first. Noises you can cause in places away from you are a good idea. Be prepared. Not only should your weapon be ready to shoot, but it's best if you have a barricade to jump behind as soon as your gun goes off. As soon as you see his muzzle flash, shoot; remember, he'll most likely do the same. Try never to stay in the same place after you shoot! Even if your target is hit and down, return fire may very well come your way.

Sighting at night is a difficult thing to do. With a gold bead front sight, the smallest amount of illumination

You lose your ability to see a target in darkness when:
1. You come into a dark building from daylight with no proper night vision preparation.
2. You're in total darkness.
3. After muzzle flash causes both eyes to shut down.

will enable you to see your front sight. That may be enough, especially if you index properly so the gun barrel is always in line with the top bone (radius) of your forearm. Remember, laser sights and lights disclose your position. Shining a flashlight into a darkened area is a terrible idea if you discover someone pointing a shotgun at you. Tritium sights enable you to get sight alignment in the dark, but in pitch black, you can't see your target anyway.

Reloaders are better pistol shots because their ammo is inexpensive. They can practice without going broke. Whether it costs a lot or a little, you need to practice. You don't need to be great--just better--and practice will keep you from being second in a contest of two.

SHOOTER LOCATOR
Muzzle flash

MUZZLE FLASH
This does two things:
1. Causes you to lose your night vision.
2. Advertises to your adversary where you are. The second after you shoot, move.

Chapter 10

HANDGUN AMMO—-STOPPING POWER

Stopping power is the smack that stops your target. Whether it's a charging bear in the woods or a knife-wielding goon on the streets, you want him to stop. Never mind whether or not he lives; you need your bullet to call a halt to his attack and thus protect your life.

With rifles and shotguns, you don't worry about stopping power much because they produce so much smack. But with pistols, energy is a critical issue. Some calibers do a better job; bullet weight and speed have a lot to do with making your bullet arrive at the target with oompah. Big caliber bullets hit with more smack because they weigh more and smack more target area. But a .44 mangl'em does <u>nothing</u> if it misses, and shooting accurately with a big handgun is extremely difficult, especially for a beginner. You wind up punching big holes in the air.

If the stopping power problem could be solved with a special bullet alone, pistol ammo manufacturers would sell thousands. In fact, some recent offerings have come close. Winchester did a great job with the Black Talon, but later pulled them off the market. Another popular seller continues to be the hydro-shock. It's a hollow point with a post in the middle which diverts target medium out to the side and thus create better bullet expansion.

The difficulty in achieving handgun stopping power arises because of variables in target density and range. Sometimes your target is behind a barricade which either stops or slows the bullet down so there is little energy for the projectile to be efficient. Heavy clothing on criminals in winter causes a hollow point to fill up with solid material. So the bullet acts more like a full metal jacket round and speeds through the target without severe wound damage. Even the complexity of an animal target contributes to the problem. If you hit a bone, more shock and damage occurs. Jacketed hollow points often fragment and move into other parts of the body to cause secondary wounds.

To achieve stopping power, you need to match the cartridge to the occasion. Big targets require heavier bullets moving along at a good rate of speed. Little rabbits, on the other hand, stop from .22 hollow points. Big bore guns mangle (Dave's father was a police inspector for many years and coined the phrase, .44 mangl'ems). That's why reloading and mix'n match loading are good ideas. You make far better ammunition than you can purchase, and some of what you can put together will NEVER be sold.

Think about this: Ammo manufacturers operate in a spirit of fear. Lawsuits now fly. Does your right to bear arms include the right to buy ammunition? Sadly, you won't find many exotic loads on the market. High velocity loads are risky. If hot coffee created a lawsuit against McDonalds, what do you think a hot bullet could cost Remington?

Therefore, you can do much better. Promise not to sue yourself and reload to make stopping power magic. Some rounds will work on one occasion; others will perform when you have other special needs. That's why mix'n match is such a big deal.

MAKING IT HAPPEN

Why do some bullets whistle straight through a target body without doing much damage? On the other hand, how come others hit like a sledge hammer?

If you shoot to produce stopping power, whatever is running toward you (a wild cougar or bear) will quit. Whoever is shooting at you will likewise quit. These are the <u>factors which determine stopping power:</u> 1. Bullet placement. 2. Penetration. 3. Size and design of the bullet. 4. Velocity. 5. Posture and status of the target.

BULLET PLACEMENT

Sirhan Sirhan shot Robert Kennedy and killed him with a .22 pistol. How could that little bullet do so much damage? Placement. He got close to Kennedy and shot him in the head. Central nervous system hits are terminal. Unless you're bullet delivers an explosive or toxic medium, placement is number one in stopping power. That's why we preach: If a handgun is too big or recoils too much, you won't be able to hit with it.

PENETRATION

You need this. The Colt .45 round I buried in a bear's fat only made him mad. Don't think a hit on any target will solve your problem. Only a bullet that keeps

> **Buy all the gun you can handle.
> Make sure you can handle
> <u>all</u> the gun you buy.**

on moving AFTER it strikes and expands deep inside the target body will create stopping power. Poorly designed bullets won't expand so whatever you shoot will continue to attack.

SIZE AND DESIGN OF BULLET

Most often, as bullet caliber increases, so does the weight. Little .22's weigh 55 grains, and big .45's go all the way up to 230 grains. For stopping power, the bigger the better---provided <u>you can deliver accurately</u>. Large caliber guns are difficult to shoot. You can buy a box of loaded cartridges or bullets for reloading that will enter a target through a half inch hole and leave a six inch exit wound. Hollow points, wadcutters, bullets with jackets--all perform differently. Without using pages of data, just do this: Ask your dealer. A well designed bullet slices through the air better so better bullet designs retain velocity at the target.

VELOCITY

If it goes fast, it penetrates. With appropriate design, it also blows tissue out to the side as it whistles through the body. The velocity multiplied by the weight determines energy---hopefully enough to expand and cause a wound cavity.

POSTURE AND STATUS OF THE TARGET

Whether man or animal, a hit from the side does more damage than from straight on. In addition to the way the target was standing, consider the target's mental state. If the target is under influence of drugs, the body will continue to fight until disability takes over.

WOUND CAVITY—-TEMPORARY

When a bullet enters a body, it creates two kinds of wound cavities—-temporary and permanent. I've received dozens of these, so I can tell you with authority. A strong Karate side kick to the torso, delivered heel first, creates a temporary wound cavity--a deep dish indentation that breaks blood vessels on the surface, bruises bone underneath, and causes swelling inside the rib cage. Sometimes, when the kick comes in under the armpit, pericardial (heart cavity tissue) is damaged. Result: the target body collapses on the ground and withers in pain. That's stopping power.

Fast moving handgun rounds deliver a temporary wound cavity with a blow worse than a karate kick. If the bullet performs according to plan, it penetrates the target's skin and then punches outward in all directions to cause a wave motion outward. **Ouch.** How hard? With a force equal to the speed of the bullet plus it's expansion ability. In slow motion, consider a balloon the size of a ball point pen entering the torso. As it slows down inside the body, it expands outward. How far? Full metal jacket bullets maintain the shape of the pen. Hollow points double up in diameter. Hydra shock rounds open sooner and wider.

Now think about the source pushing the balloon open. Though it has the capacity to open wide, an insufficient blow of air will only make it open a little. On the other hand, a gargantuan air push will open it as far as it's designed to go. The push has a name in ballistics. It's called, "kinetic energy." As long as the bullet is moving fast enough and has enough weight to shove it along and make it open through resistance, the target gets the full impact of your message.

WOUND CAVITY—-PERMANENT

Pictures from all kinds of periodicals show bullets after expansion. The muzzle velocity of the bullet divided by twelve will give you an idea how many revolutions per second the bullet turns. So when the bullet expands, the sharp edges of the jacket actually spin and buzz-saw into the target body. From that action body tissues, bones and blood vessels in the bullet path are chewed up. Immediately, bleeding occurs. Think of bleeding as an emptying out of red fluid from the body's storage facility, called blood vessels. The storage system empties, causing (hypovolemic) shock followed by death.

If the bullet you use is a fat one, the temporary wound cavity will be large. If the bullet expands rapidly to a large size, the permanent wound cavity will be extensive. To cause both of the above, however, the bullet needs to **penetrate** the target body.

Given the lowly handgun's capacity for high pressures—-and given the inability of most shooters to handle the recoil and noise from a high-velocity, heavy bullet, how can we increase penetration? Brilliant people have devoted their lives to studying the problem. The slow, big bullet group is probably in favor of the .45, and they are supported by the bullet energy dump theory, to which I subscribe. In short, I guesstimate that when a bullet with a whole bunch of energy going into the target loses all it's energy in the target, then that energy had to go somewhere. On the other end of the spectrum, bullet scientists probably came up with the super penetrating 9mm. I've reloaded these often, and been pleased with performance. Probably, the reason is this: The loss in bullet weight provides more velocity, so you get about the same result.

Finally, as with people of religious and political persuasions, anytime you have opposite ends of the spectrum, you always have middle-of-the-roaders, which very well might be the position to take. That's because some police people who were not sure which way to go disregarded the theories and concentrated on results. They kept records on all the human vermin at which their police threw lead and found out what worked best with just one hit. From their data, they determined that this is what worked best.

A. In 9mm., a 115 grain, JHP (Jacketed Hollow Point), with sufficient powder to move along at 1,200 fps.

B. Out of a .357 magnum, a 125 grain JHP out of a 4" barrel (to give the powder time to burn completely) moving along at over 1,400 fps. To be a top gun, put some of these together:

Note that the "A" round will be exiting the muzzle of automatics (with some exceptions). The "B" round comes out of your revolver. <u>I vote for the "B" round</u>, not only because it's heavier and faster, but because a .357 magnum revolver requires less skill to shoot and operate, is safe, user friendly, forgives minor maintenance neglect, isn't picky about the ammo it will shoot, <u>and also will handle the lesser, .38 Special ammo</u>, which allows a shooter to practice.

Finally, the great unknown... What's the target like? Remember, you need penetration with enough momentum to create quick expansion. You can build a round to do all that perfectly. So you load up with super-stoppers and go afield. It's winter and you discover a crime in progress. Dutifully, you fire the required two rounds into the perpetrator. He shoots back. Why? His heavy overcoat and the layers of newspaper inside his shirt slowed the bullet down. The solid material stuffed up the nose of the bullet so it couldn't expand.

Targets are always a variable. You have no way of knowing what you will encounter. Rounds that work well on rabbits don't do much against elephants, and vice versa.

For all the above reasons, we vote solidly for the mix 'n match theory of designer handloads. In this book we go to the extreme, but we want to show the outer limits of the art.

FINALLY---SOME UNKNOWNS

Of course, bullet wounds produce a psychological influence. How much depends on your customer. Many criminals out there take drugs, so they don't respond predictably to hot lead persuasion. Leaving that drug factor aside, how well you stop an attack has a lot to do with many factors. They include anger, fear of pain, preconceived notions about injury, and hatred. Most recently discovered (9/11) but probably against us for a long time are religiously motivated fanatics (See my book, ***HOW TO SURVIVE A TERROR ATTACK***). You just don't know who's out there.

SUMMARY

Understanding the terminal ballistics of handgun rounds is the key to buying ammunition that will best for your needs. When you start by considering the target (distance and kind), you can design and shoot the perfect performer. Then you can load your handgun with different loads to match the various occasions you will encounter.

You and your handgun can be the most efficient combination anywhere.

Chapter 11

COMBAT ENGAGEMENT

Engagement is the word we use to define the relationship of a man and woman who promise each other they will enter into a contract which reads in part: "Until death do us part." I suppose that's why we borrow the word and use it when we talk about a gunfight. Both ventures can be deadly.

Shakespeare might have written: "To engage, or not to engage, that is the question." The answer is: Not just "no," but heck no. Never, not even, absolutely **not**. It's OK to shoot, snipe, out range and shoot from a distance or from behind a barricade, but it's not OK to involve yourself in a shooting confrontation where there is the slightest possibility you could get shot. Gun people need to understand this. Most don't, and some who didn't are now in the hereafter. They tried hard to win and some even succeeded in eliminating the enemy--but they too-- were eliminated.

> In a gunfight competition, a tie means: Both die.

Now, listen to what irks both Dave and me. Here's a partial list of books in another publisher's catalog under the heading, COMBAT SHOOTING.
Secrets of Gunfighting. . .
Principles of Quick Kill.
Fancy shooters...
. . .Combat Handgunning
Shooting to Live
Instinct Combat Shooting
. . .Close Quarter Shooting
The movies and TV cops and robber shows also focus on you, the shooter. All of this makes enjoyable reading and viewing, but that's one reason cemeteries contain good cops. They're not with us anymore because they were beguiled by TV, silver screen and magazines, all of which <u>tell only half the story</u>! What's missing?

> **When you shoot at someone,**
> **they normally shoot back.**

To stay out of the cemetery as a customer, don't focus on shooting--as you might be fooled into doing. It's not OK to get shot **at.** Don't let it happen. Even if you only get shot, wounded and disabled, you lose.

If you stay alive, you'll be a menace to the enemy tomorrow. If you work in law enforcement, you are too valuable an asset to lose because some desk jockey thinks "you should stand up and fight like a man!" I got a better idea: I want you to live and make lots of arrests in the future.

> Two extremes in solving human conflict are:
> 1. Biblical principle.
> 2. A carefully placed charge of explosives!

It's so easy to solve human conflict in ways that provide you with a 95% chance of winning. See my two survival books, *EVERYBODY'S OUTDOOR SURVIVAL GUIDE & GREAT LIVIN' IN GRUBBY TIMES*. You can set traps, ambush, gang up and overwhelm your enemies with firepower.

Why then do so many law enforcement officers go to funerals? Adding to the list of causes of some good cops' death are some common mis-perceptions found in movies & TV.

1. Warning shots are a good idea. Even some judges believe and enforce this policy.

2. You should shoot to wound. The good guys in movies are nice guys and only wound the crooks.

3. The minute a bullet strikes a bad guy, he falls over and expires.

4. The good guy can hide behind a table, a door, a car, or a wall and not get shot.

5. You can set up a good ambush in an "H" formation (Notably done in Clint Eastwood's *Gauntlet*).

6. Once the perp is under arrest at gun point, the fight is over, even when the partner-detective steps in front of the line of fire to put the cuffs on.

7. Pistol shooters often take rifle shooters out at long distances or great heights. It's entertaining fiction, and a terrific stunt as the bad guy's stunt man does a 180° fall from a water tower.

All the above is **bull!** If you watch the movies and believe that Hollywood portrays realism, you're in for a big surprise in real life. Moreover, all of us spend more time watching TV than we do practicing shooting (or reading our Bibles). No wonder we make colossal mistakes in life! For anyone who learns handgun techniques from watching the screen, "boob tube" is the appropriate name.

The real life application of what Hollywood produces can create real danger to your health. How it really goes is this:

1. Warning shots are a good idea, but only after you've pumped a few into the perpetrator. Because of our criminal justice system's application of Hollywood to real life, saying you fired a warning shot and showing spent brass in excess of the holes in the perp's body is a fine way to leave a crime scene. In reality, firing the first (warning shot into the air) escalates the nature of the conflict to *lethal,* and anyone who shoots back after that probably would be justified in believing this was a life-threatening situation. Result: You're wounded (you hope!) and the perp gets off.

2. Shooting to wound requires the skill of John Wayne. Even if you do shoot well enough to wound, you are asking for: A. Return fire which could kill you (several police officers have been killed this way). B. A lawsuit you won't believe. Some lawyer will represent his client against you, the nazi who did this dastardly

deed to his nicely dressed client on crutches with back pain who could have been a rocket scientist someday if only he had the money (yours) for education starting with junior college. C. A clean miss; even the best shooters fail to place precision bullets sometimes. D. An enraged perpetrator on drugs who will close in on you with a contact weapon (knife, club, etc.). During the Korean war, we discovered some enemy machine gunners shot to doll rags with high power 30-06 rounds. They had continued to fire a long time after they were shot. Why? They felt no pain because enemy doctors had administered drugs before the battle.

3. Handgun bullets don't kill people unless they destroy the central nervous system. Therefore, if you get shot, shake it off and continue. If you shoot the other guy, keep on shooting! It may take him a while to feel your influence.

4. Hollywood directors know very little about live combat; many are squeamish. They confuse *cover* with *concealment*. Real bullets will fly right through most Hollywood hideouts—-especially full metal jacket slugs. Rifle bullets will penetrate trees. Standing behind a car near the driver's door will invite someone to send a round through the door and the foolhardy person taking cover behind it.

5. How stupid! With the emphasis we have on modern handguns and <u>penetrating</u> ammunition, an "H" ambush will cause good guys on either side to slice right through the target and shoot each other. This is especially true with full metal jacket ammo, which stays intact so the round whistles right on through at high speed. Any ambush with friendlies in your line of fire is stupid.

6. "Action beats reaction." This is a saying I heard many times in Special Forces, and it's absolutely true. If

you are holding a suspect within reach at gun point, he can easily take your weapon. Convicts have been observed in prison by guards practicing this move. I appeared on the G. Gordon Liddy show as a guest on my book, **CONQUER CRIME,** and Gordon told me he could easily take a handgun away from anybody (while breaking the germ's finger in the process).

7. To out class a rifle at a long distance, the pistol shooter needs: Heavy caliber at high velocity, a long sight base or an accurate scope on his pistol, an ability to hold better than a world class dam, immunity from incoming rounds, plus the kind of prayer from a righteous man that God would listen to and answer on the spot. Yeah. It could happen . . .

KING, QUEEN, KNIGHT, AND PAWN — WEAPONS

Learn about weapons' hierarchy. Just as you go up through belt levels in martial arts, weapons do the same. Basically, it goes up the ladder of lethality like this: Third: Handgun; Second: Shotgun; First: Rifle. If you engage a shotgun or rifle with only a handgun, your elevator may not go all the way to the top.

In a handgun engagement, range and caliber play an important part. Like a bully in the neighborhood against a kindergarten child, big calibers rule the roost. A .25 caliber handgun up against a .40 caliber doesn't make much sense. Therefore: <u>Armed with a pistol, engage nothing</u>. Obviously, you can see a rifle or shotgun in the hands of anybody shooting at you. If you plan to shoot your pistol at either of these weapons and you want to make a good investment, buy life insurance. Sometimes, it's difficult to tell what kind of handgun you may be up against. Big calibers go "Boom". Small ones go "Pop". Here's a good rule. **"When in doubt, get out"**. For people who only carry a small handgun around with them, figure everything out there is heavier firepower. If you can disengage, hide, take cover or run, that's better than trying a hot lead exchange.

Take this test. You and a buddy, or perhaps your wife, are out driving or camping when you both become tired so you decide to sleep at the same time. You can't find a motel or shelter in which you can hide, so you have to sleep out of doors in the open. That could be a dangerous thing to do. Each of you have a handgun and rifle, with a chambered round and full magazine. Circle your answer to these statements.

1. Yes—-No. You sleep together in your car.
2. Yes—-No. You sleep together in a tent or out in the open away from your car.
3. Yes—-No. You set your sleeping area for sound alarm in the event of an invasion into your territory.
4. Yes—-No. You sleep apart, with more than fifty yards between you.

Answers: 1. No. 2. No. 3. Yes. 4. Yes. If you answered #4 correctly, I'll forgive all other errors. The military rule: Never bunch up in enemy territory. Enemies abound in the U.S. right now. If you bunch up, then one man with a knife can get both of you. Ask Nicole Simpson.

> Had Ron Goldman ran away, Nicole would be alive. See **CONQUER CRIME**, How to be Your Own Bodyguard.

Most of the criminal goons, gangbangers, and terrorists running around don't understand firepower. Also, the focus of their life is much like that of the rats they imitate—-hide during the day and operate at night. Because of that, they <u>conceal</u> the weapons they use, which pretty much limits them to handgun.

By sleeping apart, you can cover each other with a rifle. So this is how to set up for the night. Chances of getting hit by handgun fire at more than 50 yards away are minimal. Therefore, the two of you bed down about 80 yards apart so you have clear fields of fire to each other's location. Sleep sitting up. We teach you how in *How To Be A Survivor, Book II*. Each keeps a rifle he (or she) can get quickly. Set the approach paths for sound by sprinkling the incoming trail with liberal doses of bird seed. Anyone approaching in the morning will cause the birds to flutter away so you awaken. If either of you is attacked, the other simply clears the decks with a rifle from a distance at which a pistol can hardly fight back.

<u>The key to successful engagement is in early preparation</u>. You can do several things long before you come into harm's way.

MIX 'N MATCH

Begin with a loading plan. You need to accomplish a variety of tasks with different bullets. In the event you carry one magazine with a different pattern, say, all penetrators, mark the bottom of that magazine with color—-tape or marker.

As you now know, mark your speed loaders so they match up with your cylinders when recharging, then make sure to place number #1 in the correct position as you close the cylinder. Practice this. If you don't, you may never notice that your Colt revolver cylinder spins one way and your Ruger spins the other. If you reload, you can make dummie rounds at home and spend enough time to get really quick at ejection, then loading so the color coded rounds come up to fire in proper order.

How about an engagement plan? Certain principles always apply. Others apply for daylight; still others apply for night shooting only. Muzzle flashes in the night disclose your position, so if you fail to move after you shoot, pray.

> Several cops have had weapons literally shot out of their hands while shooting in the dark around a corner. Why? The perps shot at muzzle flash.

If possible, try to get position on the high side. As a solo combatant, think of a barricade as your best friend. It may be hard for you to move without getting shot at.

Partners, however, should seldom stay in the same location. Maneuver as soon as you can. Without exposing yourself to fire, climb a hill, get on a roof top, get into the upper floors of a parking lot or building. With superior elevation, you have better protection, better view and a wider field of fire.

Grouted brick walls are best. Thick hardwood will stop most handgun bullets. In your home, a mattress with newspaper in thick layers taped to the bottom and pulled up on it's side will stop a lot of calibers. The best and cheapest for a permanent position like your home would be sandbags.

Some gunfights happen so fast you simply react without thinking. Most often in law enforcement, fast gunfights are settled with one or two rounds. In war or defense work, however, the gun fights last a lot longer and the rules of engagement don't dictate that you have to wait for the other guy (criminal) to make the first move. In those kinds of encounters, evaluate your chances as soon as you get the opportunity.

You develop tactics by gathering intelligence on your enemy's capability. In other words, what's he shooting? Did you hear a light pop or a big boom? How far away is the shooter? Can you move quickly to cover? Know your shooting capability perfectly well. You need to know you can shoot accurately "this far" and one of your bullets penetrates "this much."

Obviously, the crack of a speeding bullet overhead followed by a big boom is something you never want to hear. We teach you in my book, *THE RIFLE RULES*, precisely how to locate shooter's location. If all you have with you is a handgun, however, don't even bother. A handgun against a rifle is like a girl in a fight against Mike Tyson. Running for cover would be the best idea—-not away in a straight line either.

WEAPONS MATCHED EVENLY

Not so obvious will be the even fights, in which both weapons are the same but you think you can out shoot the germ. With no cover available, at least pop into a "smaller target" position. Pin down the target with enough fire so you can move. Be careful with trigger control. That's the first thing to go under pressure. Slow, steady fire into the target location will produce better. Think about ricochets. If your target is hiding behind rocks, or in a doorway built out of stone, a couple of billiard ricochet shots with full jacket round noses may ruin his day.

HOW MANY SHOOTERS IN YOUR PARTY?

If you work alone all the time, either as a woodsman or police officer, your tactical focus is on survival. It isn't necessary to subdue your enemy. Simply make sure you stay alive. Call 911. Get some help. Don't take chances or try to be a posthumous hero. Even if the bad guy escapes, he will be caught. Stay alive and testify at his trial. With a partner, however, you can be more aggressive.

HANDGUN COMBAT IN PAIRS

First rule: Never shoot together at the same rate so you empty your weapons simultaneously (down time=death). Don't bunch up. Staying apart will keep you both alive. Even if one of you gets shot and the shooter disengages, the other can patch up the hole and get help.

Since you will be shooting from separate and distant positions, be careful about your fields of fire. People in

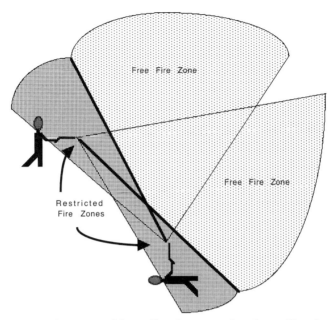

the same Army accidentally shoot each other. Don't you do the same. If apart, make sure you have restricted fields of fire---a no-shoot area in which your partner is located. Change locations? Tell your partner. That's one reason why the little two way radios are such a critical item. If you don't have a verbal way of communication, hand signals will have to do. I guarantee you, however, that during a raging gunfight, they are a poor second. Without being able to tell your partner, make sure neither of you moves into the other's free fire zone.

As you now know, handguns are the worst tools of engagement. Nobody ever died because they ducked behind good cover and stayed out of harm's way. Of course, if your job is catching and imprisoning scum, you may have to shoot. In such an event, never go up against a superior weapon, keep your own exposure to a minimum, and try to operate at a range father away than your opponent can shoot accurately or effectively.

Engagement with weapons where the other party has the slightest chance of hitting you must be avoided at all cost. If the situation forces you to engage, then at least get into it with superior weaponry. On the other hand...

Stay alive and holy. It beats dead and holey by a bunch. If you engage with a small caliber against a big bore gun, shoot from an incorrect range against a long-range shooter, or expose your body to incoming, you are flirting with death.

Chapter 12

INCOMING
The Art and Science of Getting Shot <u>At!</u>

Dave and I believe it's a rip-off tragedy if we don't teach you this. In all of the violent movies and TV shows we see, the good guy wins. Even if he gets shot, it's "just a scratch". Of course, we all identify with the shooter—-the good guy who wins the shoot-out and rides off with the Hollywood honey.

Likewise, Dave and I are further aggravated by the print media's focus on shooting. Draw this; sight on that; blast the bad guys. You'll see pictures of all kinds of shooters winning the gun battles.

WHAT YOU NEVER SEE BUT MUST CONSIDER

If you draw your handgun, chances are more than decent someone else will have a similar gun pointed at you. In fact, politicians have created some terrible rules of engagement. You have to wait until you feel your life is threatened before you can respond, and you can't respond with any more force than that which was facing you. Therefore, you can't go around with your gun drawn.

That's why the unconventional presentation is such a good idea. You need to have your hand on your weapon and be ready to shoot if you sense danger. Later you either remove your hand from the gun (still concealed) or you shoot as soon as you find out that the threat you suspected becomes a reality.

Now follow this line of thought: You can't use more force than someone uses on you. You can only shoot when you are faced with the threat of losing life. If you do draw your handgun, the other guy certainly has a right to fear for his life, so you've just elevated a conflict to a lethal level. Therefore, isn't it logical to believe... <u>Any time you resort to handgun force, it's highly probable someone will shoot at you?</u>

Knowing this, why is it that nobody has instructed you on how to get shot? Granted, it <u>ain't</u> fun to read and think about. But learning how to shoot the other guy is only half what you need to know. If we don't give you some advice on this vital subject, we don't do our jobs as writers. Thus we get to: Incoming 101, The Art and Science of Getting Shot At. Here's the course synopsis: DON'T!

Simply telling you "don't get shot" may not work. Since the ACLU has gone to court and relieved the overcrowding in prisons, society now is overcrowded

> **San Francisco Shoot Out**
> Over 100 rounds were fired. Whacko wants to play "The news will make you famous." He decides to make an impression on the world through sensational media. Dead: Suspect and one officer. Wounded: One officer and one citizen.
> Dead officer was shot while trying to reload a revolver. The wounded officer was barricaded behind a house wall. Suspect merely used a rifle (probably with FMJ ammo) and shot through the wall to wound the officer.
> Although the suspect was shot with Treasury load .38 Special, his bullet proof vest stopped the slug. Finally, a police sniper with a rifle had enough power to penetrate the vest.

with criminals. Every state in the union now contains tens of thousands of these germs running loose in society. In California, for example, the figure is 82,000. Police can't touch one of them until **after** he commits a crime. So you certainly could get shot at.

Perhaps we think they'll miss and we won't. Again, that may not happen. Guys who shoot at you may not be great pistol marksmen, but they often carry guns with firepower enough (12 or more rounds stacked in a magazine) to let lead fly all over in your general direction. You'll probably be scared. Adrenaline tends to make us shake, which isn't helpful when trying to hold your sights steady. The guy on the other side may not be shaking as badly. Drugs and alcohol might have given him an "I don't care" attitude. Even if you put a hole in his body, he may not feel it. He has nothing to lose. Prison is no deterrent. All of his friends are there. His weapon is unregistered; if he kills you, he can discard it or give it back to the owner from whom he rented it to commit the crime.

So chances are good that you will be shot at. First, let's think about skipping the event. Since bad guys can't hit what they can't see, hiding is a good idea. If possible, let's dive behind a barricade. Once safe, you can solve this gunfight problem.

You need to understand the difference between cover and concealment. A bullet stopping barricade provides cover. This is the definition of concealment: Anything through which the other guy's bullet might travel, even though it hides you. Wood fences and some trees, for example, are not cover. House walls are poor. Anything easily penetrated by any flying projectile provides only concealment.

Here's a life-saving rule: If you're only concealed during a fire fight, shoot and move. Moving is absolutely necessary because the opposition will shoot at your muzzle flash or the sound of gunfire. Stay concealed, but be looking for bullet-stopping cover. Likewise, check to see if you can't penetrate what your opponent believes is cover. (You'll be able to load some great penetrating surprises).

How does one shoot? Sight. He sees you, then he aims and pulls the trigger. How else might he sense your presence? Sound. It's a relative thing. When you either make more noise than he or camp next to a noisemaker while he's slightly less noisy, you can't hear him. Don't use earphones for any entertainment in a high burglary area. You can't hear a door hinge squeak. Is there another way? Smell. We don't use that in the city too much, but in the woods we pick up campfire scents, cigarette smoke (I've smelled it a mile away) and perhaps human odor.

So now you enter into conflict. Success or failure depends on his and your **human senses.** Knowing that, how could you win? Here it is:

> **Diminish or take away his senses
> while strengthening yours.**

That was my function in Special Forces. We fooled the enemy when we all looked like bushes. Camouflage kept him from seeing us. He couldn't hear us because we taped our dog tags, oiled our boots, and stayed away from naturally noisy places such as moving water. We also were very careful in terrain that might bounce sound. We buried all of our body wastes--both kinds. To summarize: Nobody could see us, hear us, or smell us-- we took away the enemy's senses

Let's apply the principle to you. First, don't wear bright clothes at night. As anybody knows, certain fabrics reflect light to a greater degree than others. In law enforcement, the policy might call for white shirts and ties. Therefore, wear a dye-darkened undershirt and immediately lose the white shirt and ornaments as soon as combat begins.

Second, let the other guy work in the light. Stay in the shadows as much as possible. Don't move. Wait for him to move. Hiding in shadows provides a good advantage, especially if you can move <u>undetected</u> from one shadow to another. A difference between the light intensity in which he's positioned and your own darkness will often enable you to win. Light up the outside yards in your home. You can buy lights with sensor switches that turn on and flood the area like a stage when anyone walks under them.

<u>Keep your eyes night-operational!</u> If you use a campfire at night, wear an eye patch over your gun-sighting eye. It takes a long time before your eye's iris

expands so you can see in the dark, but it only takes a quick second to make it close down. If you've been staring into a campfire with both eyes, any idiot can deal with you from outside and you won't be able to see him. Also, don't stare into city light sources at night. Close at least your gun sighting eye to bright lights aimed in your direction; that way you maintain your night vision.

What about sound? How could you enhance theirs and make yours minimal? In your own area, you set the ground so that anything moving makes noise. Broken glass in his area provides you with valuable intelligence which you don't have to see. Gravel pits outside your windows go "crunch" the minute someone steps there. Inside a building, take off your shoes so you make no sound.

> The most fundamental concept of tactics goes like this: You analyze the enemy's capability. You learn during practice and training exactly what you can do. Then you match what you got against what he ain't.

Want to improve your sense of both smell and hearing? Get a dog. Dogs can smell a stranger. I often used my dog as a pillow in the woods. I kept her warm; she stayed on guard. On several occasions, she growled lightly to wake me up because of a bear or coyote upwind. I had my .41 mag ready long before anything came close to camp.

Stay upwind and trust your nose. You really will be able to smell a guy who is sweating because gunfighting makes everybody nervous. It also creates gastric disturbance. Your upwind enemy may deliver scent signals that lead right to him. Now, let's make the other guy easier to see. You need to sense him better than he can sense you. Then the battle advantage is yours. Out in the field in a clear cut you can dig a trench across a likely enemy approach and fill it with dry wood, then douse it with diesel fuel. If the enemy gets inside that line, you touch it off with a remote ignition device. Result: All the bad guys will be backlit, and you get to shoot silhouettes.

When all is said and done, if they can't see, hear or smell you, but you can detect them, you'll be safe.

You have choices, a couple of which are: Shoot first and best, or dive for cover. Probably, cover is the best choice. Cover keeps you safe. Shooting is risky for 2 reasons. A. You disclose your location and expose part of your body. B. You may hit--only to be sued afterwards. So a quick move to cover is best.

However, what if cover isn't available? As your drill sergeant, I gotta first ask, "Why weren't you operating near cover?" You don't have to run down the middle of a street. Near buildings you can always jump into a doorway or hide behind a parked car, etc. This is the way I want you to be: Outstanding in your field. That's one word; not two. Don't be out, standing in your field. Nevertheless, what if someone tries to shoot you while you're in the middle of nowhere?

Don't forget the theory of relative target size. Shrink your body. Shoot a lot.

Given equal shooting ability and equal firepower, you double your chances of hitting first if you simply get your target size.

To make your defense complete, consider what you might do if you can't get to either concealment or cover, and you don't want to shrink your body. Wear protection. A variety of body armor is available which will keep almost all handgun slugs from penetrating your body. Even a thick book taped to a shirt over your heart could save your life.

Contrary to what you see in the movies, you can take a hit and live. Many people think handgun wounds are fatal, but lots of people who were shot are alive and well today.

UNNECESSARY HANDGUN DEATHS

People die after being shot by handgun for one of two reasons. A. The bullet destroys their body physiologically. Most often that's a CNS hit. B. They kill themselves psychologically. "A" doesn't happen very often. "B" happens a lot. If you're alive and bleeding, you didn't die---and you won't—-as long as you remain calm and get some decent medical attention. The single exception is a CNS (Central Nervous System) hit, in which event, you won't feel it anyway. Don't let your brain send you to judgement before your time.

DEVELOP AN UNBEATABLE ATTITUDE

Become invincible. It's a state of mind as well as body. Special Forces people often develop a life-preserving attitude. The training is such a bear that people who survive it really believe *nothing* can kill them. You don't have to employ those methods of severe self training, although I recommend them. If you can, train hard. Keep your body in top shape and your mind clear. Learn gun play by rote with frequent practice. If you should get into a shoot out, you need to shoot back, move, seek cover, and don't forget to count shots. Assess your situation. With all the facts known, you'll be able to plan and then use the perfect bullet. "Perfect" is <u>the one</u> that solves your problem.

As far as attitude goes, just remember this, <u>it ain't over</u>. You may be down and bleeding, but that's the best time to get tricky and get even. Never even think about giving up. If you are losing this confrontation, get mad and fight back! "The best defense is a good offense".

<u>GUNFIGHT PRIORITIES--A CHECKLIST</u>

A. Before it even starts. Plan. You know your areas of operation. Think, "what will I do if . . ."

B. Eliminate the possibility of getting hit. Take cover. Perhaps destroy enemy ability to deliver fire. Consider the stopping power of your own ammunition. A round with good penetrating ability can make all the difference.

C. If no cover, concealment helps. Use concealment when cover is inadequate, but don't stay in one place. The first time you shoot, you advertise your vulnerable hiding place.

D. Engage only if necessary. When should you engage? Only when you know you can neutralize the threat without risk to your own person. Never let anger or fear be the basis of any decision. Those two emotions cause soldiers to charge machine gun nests with pistols---and win medals---posthumously.

E. If you possibly can, identify his weaponry as soon as it starts. Stay where you are. When you know you can hit at the enemy's range, then, maybe <u>engagement</u> will be a relatively safe thing to do. Find out for sure in the next chapter.

SHOOTING VICTIMS
HOW THEY GOT TO THE HOSPITAL

They . . .

1. were "situation blind." They didn't pay attention to the people around them or what was going on.

2. thought crime would never happen to them.

3. never developed a "fight back" attitude.

4. believed that everyone is a good person. (Freud's idea, not the Bible's).

5. never owned, carried or used an offensive weapon, such as a gun, knife, walking stick or club.

6. believed the police would keep them safe.

With no help around, at least shrink your body size as you shoot. The smaller target you present, the less likelihood of your becoming ventilated. Nobody likes to think of getting shot <u>AT</u>, but failure to consider the possibility will cause lack of knowledge and zero preparation. Knowing what to do and being prepared to do it can save a handgunner's life.

> I find reloading to be a mentally relaxing activity. Once I'm in the swing of it, it relieves stress.
> Dave

Chapter 13

WHY RELOAD?

We don't want you to own a weapon for which you can't make your own ammunition unless it's rimfire. Don't buy another gun until you have the capability to reload for the ones you already own. If you have to, sell one gun and spend that money to set yourself up in the ammunition business.

Ammunition is easy to make and you can do it just about anywhere. I have resolved to carry a Lee Loader anytime I go hunting. Mr Hodgdon told me personally that his powders could be stored successfully for over 20 years. You can buy enough primers to shoot for a lifetime for a small investment. You can cast or swage your own bullets and store them. Reloading is not a difficult skill to learn! However, it's a vital skill you can learn, practice and enjoy to get the best and cheapest security possible. With this skill, you can survive. Without it, you may have to use your gun as a club.

Below, you'll find good reasons why you need to reload. The number one reason—more important than any of them—-is: What might the anti-gun people in this country try next?

Ban ammunition!

Could it happen? One Senator proposed a 1,000% percent tax on ammo. (Smart idea; then only rich kids could afford it, like drug dealers.) In Los Angeles, during the riots, the city government shut down sales of ammunition. (Another bright idea; the rioters already had all they needed. Good citizens were left defenseless.)

To make sure you will have ammo in the future, "forever," you need to learn to reload your own.

Want additional reasons?

1. The key to stopping power out of your handgun is penetration and bullet expansion. That maximum stopping power requirement changes with weather, circumstances, barricades and range. Different shooting situations require different loads. Certain kinds of bullets will penetrate a barricade. Handloaders can solve those problems. Perhaps you'll make the bullet harder by dropping hot lead into quenching water or by using a different metal such as pewter. Think about using a lead bullet as a sabot with a super hard center. When the lead stops at a barricade, the super center keeps on flying (see number 10).

2. To be a great pistol shot, you have to practice, which will cost you a bundle if you buy ammunition in a store. Reloading drastically reduces the cost of shooting because reloading components cost less than manufactured ammo. (You don't have to pay your own products liability—-just promise not to sue yourself.)

3. You'll develop superb accuracy. Furthermore, if you <u>do</u> miss, you'll know it was **not** the fault of weapon or cartridge. Confidence in your ammo is an important step in becoming a first class shot.

4. Our forms enable you to keep good records and tie reload data to measured performance. Therefore, nothing leaves your muzzle without your knowing exactly what it will do. You can also duplicate a special high performance load anytime you want. Just refer to your form book.

5. Eventually, I believe the economy of this country will fail completely. You'll need a marketable skill, and just about the time everyone loses a job, the need for ammunition will drastically increase. If the country fails, an overpowering increase in crime (as they have in Russia) will keep the demand for ammunition high.

6. When you load your own, you can achieve higher velocities. That means harder hitting with better terminal ballistic performance.

7. Anybody knows you can work up a load which works well in your particular weapon. You may need higher velocity out of a short barrel. Muzzle flash may tell everyone where you are. Fast burning powders help to solve both problems.

8. A customized load can eliminate flinching. When your handgun hurts you (both ears and body) you'll never hit anything. Reloaders fix this by using a lighter powder charge and a less heavy bullet. With comfort you get control. You'll place bullets with precision.

9. You'll be able to out-shoot other pistol shooters at long distances. More powder pushing a bullet with a better ballistic coefficient will increase your area of influence. Think also about choosing a bullet with a high coefficient. They slide through the air with less resistance.

10. Reloaders have the option of making custom ammunition with modified projectiles. Why not use lead as a sabot? Why not think of a bullet as a delivery vehicle? Bullets can be drilled in the nose and filled with foreign substances. Why use plastic for the only covering of a sabot projectile? You can use lead as well. If you drill the nose out of a lead bullet and insert hard steel, brick walls will no longer be safe barricades for criminals.

11. Finally, getting started in reloading cost you little and sometimes, you actually save money in the beginning. Why? If you reload, you don't need to buy an expensive weapon. The money you save on the purchase of a weapon will often be enough to set you up in reloading style. Lots of practice will enable you to shoot a cheap gun like a pro. Special loads often make cheaper guns deliver lead like expensive ones.

Don predicts: There will come a time soon in this country when your weapons will be the only thing between you and peril. Learn to reload. Both Dave and I want you to be A HAPPY HANDGUNNER.

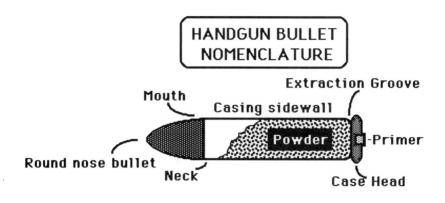

Chapter 14

MAKING HANDGUN AMMUNITION

When you shoot a gun, you pop a primer, burn powder to shove a bullet forward and slam the case body outward into the chamber's walls. When you reload, you un-shoot. Put back together the stuff you just fired. Resize the case; then add three new components:

A new primer. Note: Commercial primers don't fit in military brass. A primer pocket reamer resizes the pocket so commercial primers fit.

A precision measured load of powder for the weight of the bullet you'll use,

A projectile for a particular job. Maybe you want your bullet to expand, penetrate, or spread shot.

When you put new components together, they'll make a cartridge much better than the commercial one you may have shot. Your powder measure will be perfectly accurate and the projectile you choose will do a much better job at certain distances than any you can find in stock ammo.

START WITH THE BRASS CASE

The brass is often dirty and may have defects. Why screw things up with dirty cases? Clean your cases with chemical cleaners like Birchwood Casey, 0000 steel wool and a rag, or--the best and easiest way—-by tumbling. Clean the primer pocket by hand and at the same time, check for defects.

> The rule for used brass is:
> **When in doubt; toss it out.**

Cases stretch and thicken at their necks after several firings. Check case length with a gauge and if needed, trim the case mouth to make sure it's not too long. Firearms chambers are made to close tolerances so cases can't be too long or thick. Keep your re-sized cases in separate lots according to how many times they've been fired.

Discard all cases with split necks, body cracks, over-sized primer pockets, and bad dents. Check carefully on old or well-used brass for the thinning mark around the base of the case; otherwise you may suffer case-head separation.

SETTING A NEW PRIMER

We use boxer primers; they go into a primer pocket with a single (not a double) flash hole. Make sure the primer pocket is clean, and press-fit-by-feel a new primer into the pocket. Over push and you may seat a primer too deep in the pocket. Result: The firing pin can't strike hard enough; you created a dud. If you don't push hard enough, the primer dimples out of the case shell. You can either buy a gauge to get it just right or use close eyesight to make sure the primer is flush (on the same level) with the back of the case.

GUN POWDER

Powder comes in various burn rates---some fast---others slower. When you buy powder, get the manual which tells you exactly how much powder to use with a given bullet weight. Once you have discovered a powder-measured charge that weighs exactly as much as you need, you can use your powder measure without weighing each and every charge. To drop accurate loads use ball powder; it meters best. Extruded and flake powders often break and then jam the working parts of a powder measure.

For any law enforcement or military person, muzzle flash is a problem so match the burn rate of the powder to the barrel of the gun you shoot. That will keep blast and flash from being troublesome. If you shoot a revolver, you might choose a fast burning powder so residue doesn't lodge under the star extractor and thus restrict it from seating. That's terrible news; the cylinder won't close. Hodgdon makes a "Universal Clays" powder that just about solves this problem.

CHOOSING BULLETS

Choices are: Buy commercial or cast your own. People who make commercial bullets do a fantastic job. They've researched, tried and tested a kazillion projectiles. Some of theirs open quickly; others penetrate well. Still others have excellent ballistic coefficients.

The majority of pistol ammo is fired in practice. Think economy. Practice with cheap lead. Use fancy high-priced bullets for doing business. Try to keep your lead practice slugs and your business bullets as close as you can to the same weight and velocity.

Learning to cast bullets is becoming popular. If you mould your own, you should obtain a bullet mould of the same weight as your commercial, jacketed counter part. Store your bullets in air tight containers to avoid oxidation, especially lead bullets.

RELOADING EQUIPMENT

Many people often begin reloading with a portable reloading outfit they can stash or carry. With a few thousand primers, some powder and shot, you can make gun food forever. When you begin reloading, you may reload in the kitchen due to lack of space. With normal growth and expansion, you'll become an involved handloader. You can get faster reloading presses, more expensive scales, tumblers to clean brass better and a chronograph to keep track of increasing bullet speeds.

TOTAL PORTABILITY

For the back packer, space conscious survivalist, or anyone who wants to reload at the range, a portable outfit works well. The Lee hand presses have enough leverage to full-length resize cases and perform all reloading operations. It's most economical. In the field, a charge cup measures powder charges.

THE PRESS

No matter whether semi-portable or fixed to a bench only Godzilla could lift, the press is the back bone of the ammo making operation. It holds reloading dies, the shell holder and primer arm. Some presses, with revolving turrets that move a cartridge from one step of the reloading operation to another, have places for a complete set of dies, a powder measure, and an automatic primer feeder. They produce ammo much faster.

RELOADING BOOKS

You absolutely need a loading manual or two, preferably with a name brand to match the jacketed bullets you buy. Those manuals contain the keys to good bullet choices. Some list coefficients so you know right away how well your bullet will whistle through the air. Of course, the weight of the bullet is critical. For each bullet weight, the all-important information on powder charge weight tells you precisely what to drop in the case.

RELOADING DIES

When you shove a brass case into a die, you reduce its expanded (by gunpowder pressure during firing) size to fit your chamber. Hardened steel dies are made in sets for a specific cartridge. Pistol dies come three to a set. The first die has the same function as the #1 rifle die; it sizes and de-primes. The second die's expander plug flares open the mouth of the case. The third die crimps the case around the seated bullet.

> **Avoid case lube. All major reloading companies offer carbide dies for handgun calibers. We recommend them.**

ABOUT CRIMPING

The roll crimp die is better for revolver cartridges because it rolls the mouth of the case into the outside of the bullet to hold the bullet firmly. Thus, heavy recoil doesn't dislodge a bullet from the case while it rests either in a cylinder or magazine before it comes up to fire. To adjust a seating die to crimp a revolver bullet, back the die out two turns (1/8") from the face of the shell holder.

Taper dies squeeze the case against the bullet, leaving the case mouth straight for chambering and head spacing in auto pistols.

WEIGHING POWDER

A powder scale is essential. If you go to the field with only a charge cup, that's OK, but you must know the exact weight of a full cup of powder. After weighing the charge to find out, don't change powders in the field!

The most widely used and acceptable powder scales are the balance type. The best scales have knife edge beams and magnetic dampening for perfect balance. Powder scales must be leveled before weighing. Don't set the scale up in a windy place; the slightest breeze can make the wrong powder charge look right. Electronic scales cost 3 to 6 times the price of a good balance type, but they eliminate balance scale problems.

A powder funnel is indispensable for filling cartridge cases or returning unused powder to its proper container. Buy a see-through plastic funnel designed for reloaders and a powder trickler so you can drop powder one grain at a time.

Never take your powder measure's accuracy for granted. Weigh the powder always to make sure it's dropping accurate measurements. A good procedure: Adjust the powder measure until it drops the exact weight. Then drop 10 charges. Stop. Drop a charge into the powder scale pan and check it. OK? Continue. After using the powder measure make sure to empty it completely. Mixing powders is disastrous for your health.

POWDER TEMPERATURES

Temperatures can effect a powders burning rate and in turn raise chamber pressures. Tight bores and chambers can compound this situation. If you load your ammo at 50 degrees Fahrenheit and then shoot it at 70 degrees, the difference is not noticeable. But when the temperature reaches 100 degrees plus (Arizona desert), chamber pressures also start climbing. At 105 degrees Fahrenheit, pressure rise will be noticeable, and at 140°, major changes will occur to powder. If you're going to shoot in a hot climate reduce your load by 2 grains of powder to be safe.

OTHER EQUIPMENT FOR RELOADING

Blocks with 50 holes, made of wood or plastic, are necessary for holding cases upright during the reloading process. Be careful when you use these. Don't stop powder charging in the middle of a row. Move down a row of empty cases IN ONE DIRECTION ONLY. Accept zero interruptions from phone, family, etc.

When a case sticks in your reloading die, you usually pull the rim off your case. To remove it you need a stuck case remover. Don't try to pound or pull a stuck case out of a die; use the right tool so you don't damage your equipment.

The best bullet pullers work in your reloading press so you don't pull bullets without damaging the case or spilling powder.

A micrometer, or vernier caliper, either dial or digital, is indispensable to a reloader. Any time you want a measurement of case or bullet, you'll need one or the other. Do not buy a cheap plastic caliper. Get a good one for high quality ammunition.

SPECIALIZED AMMUNITION

I wouldn't ask you to worry if this weren't important. But for this I need you to be paranoid. Handguns are sensitive to excess pressure. Also, many autos are real

> All the media noise and hype about armor piercing bullets is nothing. Anybody can make one. The trick is in drilling the nose; you need to use a lathe because the key issue is concentricity.

finicky about the ammunition they **refuse to** shoot. The most important aspect of any handgun ammunition is reliability, especially for business gun users. Many high-ticket bodyguards have a reloading room and the knowledge to make some rounds King Kong would be proud of. What do they use? "Commercial ammunition; all from the same lot number."

Never carry ammunition into the field you haven't tested. In handgun work, you have to know your ammo works. Your life depends on it.

You can just about reload any cartridge case to exceed factory ammo performance. Furthermore, you can get creative and make some rounds for yourself that you might never find on the market. A word of caution when you do, however. Go slowly. Do things a step at a time. Use our forms to tie performance to the load so you can check back. **Do not** exceed published maximums. Basically, you're matching powder against bullet weight; too much of either can cause excessive pressures in your gun. Weigh both components. Increase your loads in small, safe steps.

SHORT BARRELED DEFENSE LOADS

For the two inch revolver, we like the idea of using a hollow based wadcutter. Shove it into the case backwards. Thus you create the biggest hollow point available for the .357 magnum or .38 Special. In tests, we've recovered bullets which were flattened out to look like quarters. Of course, penetration is minimal. If you use only commercial ammunition and you want a load to work well out of a 2" barrel, try SWCHP's (Semi Wadcutter Hollow Points).

DUPLEX LOADS

It's like an after-holiday sale. Shoot one, get another one free! With a duplex load you get two projectiles flying ahead for the price of one powder load. Use a gas check over the powder charge so it won't get mixed up with your projectiles. Try bore-diameter lead balls. You may want to use a bullet and ball load. If so, load the bullet (less wind resistance) in front of the ball. Be careful. You have to add up total projectile weight in order to choose the right powder charge. You can probably go as high as (total) 200 grains with .38/.357 cases, but velocity will be low and close distance bullet strike will be high (probably due to muzzle flip).

LEAD SABOTS

Who needs plastic? You can cast your own sabots out of lead. Then just drill the center---precisely. Off-center drillings (one thousandth of an inch off) will create a spinning bullet with too much weight on one side. Result, the thing spirals away from the muzzle and flies like a wild duck.

Once you use a lathe and drill a hole exactly in the center, you can insert all kinds of things in the hollow point up front. An insert of pewter or a small BB made from hard steel will probably penetrate an engine block.

HANDGUN SHOT LOADS

Keep your powder charge on the light side to keep from blowing the shot charge apart. Since short barreled guns have less rifling to interfere with shot patterns, we like this load for the shorty. Use a gas check or paper wad to keep the powder and shot separated. Cut and use a thin felt pad to cushion the shot. I also use an inverted gas check as a top wad, and a heavy roll crimp to hold it all together. With a rifled pistol barrel, shot loads are good only up to 10 feet. As you probably know, shot cartridges are also factory made and offered almost everywhere. Called snake loads, they work well on rattlers. Human snakes also respond, so many carry these as first up in a mix 'n match loading.

COOKIE CUTTERS

These are sold commercially by PMC in most sporting goods stores. They are solid copper and have a hole in each end. The idea: Whistle through the target body with over-penetration and create bleeding wounds---both at entrance and exit. Bullet weight: only 67 grains. Speed: Over 1,800 fps. If the bullet doesn't get you, the heat trail might make you sneeze.

THE FRENCH ARCANE

How would you like a fast mover that collapses and moves right on through the target? Sold mostly in France, the .357 variety speeds along faster than 2,000 fps! It is 70 grains of solid copper, concave and pointed.

***

From the variety of ammo on the market, you don't have to think very far ahead to know that you can make almost all the same stuff at home. Make multiple copies of the form we provide to keep excellent records. Increase bullet weights and powder charges in small steps. Then, once you find the load that works well for your handgun, stock up.

Chapter 15

RELOADING SAFETY

KEEP ACCURATE RECORDS. In my early reloading days, I failed to do this once. I got terrific performance out of a certain box of cartridges, but I couldn't duplicate them. Also, some rounds I reloaded were terrible. **Keep detailed records!** Otherwise you won't be able to reproduce the same formula performers. Likewise, rounds that fly out in space worse than star trekkies can't be avoided.

If you get a round that surprises you or is unusual, stop. Don't shoot any more from that lot (bunch of rounds you put together) until you discover why.

Usually, that means going back to the bench and pulling the rounds apart. Are you sure what kind of powder you used? If not, incinerate it (the powder, not the whole cartridge).

Make super sure you <u>know what you are using</u>. If you repackage any powder into your own container, you are setting yourself up for a huge mistake.

Consider the gain vs. the risk. You can save a few cents by reusing a damaged case. A new eye is priceless. Examine every case and hull you will reload. Damage of any kind? Chuck it. That also goes for any powder or primer you are not sure about. You **must know** the exact powder and primer you are using. Otherwise, throw it out.

With the exception of <u>one</u> container of powder, <u>one</u> box of primers, and <u>one</u> box of projectiles, the reloading bench must be CLEAN! Failing to do that can cost the price of a new gun.

Drink alcohol while you reload? Terrible idea. You need far more presence of mind when you put primer and powder together than when you drive a car. If you drink, you probably smoke, too. When one hot ash lands on gunpowder, the resulting flash fire will burn too much, too fast.

Use ammunition loaded by others if you believe waiting for a double powder charge to go off is exciting. Those who casually sell their reloaded ammunition may not know what they're doing. Just think of the fun you could have by shooting someone's ammo when they don't know that seating a bullet too deep into a casing can put pressure on the powder—-enough to cause an explosion.

Sorry—-no children in the reloading area or room unless supervised and quiet. You can't afford distractions. You'll need to concentrate on precise & repetitive routines. Some children like to put 165 grain bullets in with 150's. It's also fun to put one of those little pieces of shot down in a primer cup. The rule is: Only highly <u>competent</u> adults get to place hands anywhere near the presses or components.

Keep component storage at correct temperature and humidity ranges.

Don't take reloading data from any source other than a reloading book or the manufacturer of the component. They pay close attention and they edit carefully. Writers, on the other hand, could easily try to type a "3" but hit a "4".

Vehicles, planes and weapons all have operating limits. If you drive faster than a vehicle was designed to be driven, you either blow up the engine or crash. Planes come out of the sky hard when the wings break off. Weapons have limits too. You can't make one shoot high velocity pushing too heavy a bullet without causing damage. Sometimes you also destroy the shooter. Reload **only** for performance within the limitations of the gun. Automatics are sensitive to powder variations. Too little and they fail to feed. Too much and the slide comes back with excessive force.

Want to die? Try reloading in a hurry. This endeavor requires that you spend the time to be precise.

Don't think weighing the same powder charge twice is dumb; it can be a life-saver. If you ever load anything close to a maximum load, hand weigh each charge. Develop a list of procedures you <u>always</u> follow. Example. Weigh charge, check book, double check bullet weight for this charge. Set powder measure. Re-weigh charge. OK? Now, run twenty cases under the measure. Let <u>nobody</u> interrupt you while dropping powder! If your wife wants to know if there are anymore fritos, tell her, "Look under the sofa cushions by yourself."

Watch to make sure no (humid) powder sticks in the drop tube. Visually inspect each powder-loaded case.

Use a flashlight to make sure that the powder is at the same level. Stop. Throw another powder charge and weigh it. Is the weight still the same?

Instead of making the gun do a little more, you do it. Stalk better and get closer to what you have to shoot. The practice will be good for you. Work on your body scent, noise discipline and camouflage to get game to come in closer to you. If you find that you need to shoot from a longer distance, **don't try to cure the problem with too big a load!** Buy a magnum.

For purposes of this book, we want you to learn to reload, with no danger to yourself or teammates. Therefore, start with a load velocity and bullet weight in the lower end of the spectrum. Keep improving your loading techniques and test your rounds until you know for sure what every weapon does.

Use our reload/performance form. Copy 50 (we give you the release) and have them spiral bound. Those forms give you the records you need to go back to the bench and duplicate your best results.

Once you find a round that works perfectly in your weapon and provides the smack you can be proud of--- make it yours forever.

Chapter 16

CASTING YOUR OWN BULLETS

If you buy projectiles from Sierra, Hornady, etc., you get the result of fine engineering research. Modern bullets made in America are superb. That's probably why they are so expensive.

Want cheap bullets? Cast your own. Besides being an inexpensive way to get gun food, it's a valuable skill to learn. If your government can restrict the sale of ammunition, why not do the same with bullets?

Another fine reason for learning how is this: Some of the bullets you will make for special purposes cannot be found in any store. You can buy bullet molds from Lyman to make bullets that do magic. If a store sold them, some attorney would probably sue them into bankruptcy.

A NOTE ON CASTING SAFETY

You will be dealing with lead. It's not only harmful to those into whom you inject it via gun muzzle, but it's also bad for you---to breathe. Everybody dies anyway, but the guys who either breathe lead or catch some in a gunfight go to judgement earlier than normal. Melt lead in a well-ventilated area, and use a fan to blow the fumes away from you into the air. Hot lead on bare skin is likewise uncool. So wear heavy foot wear, gloves, apron and eye protection. Be extremely cautious about letting children into the casting area!

Note that we don't discuss swaging here. That's because the cost for swaging equipment out-weighs savings. Even so, swaged bullets perform better than their inferior lead cousins, so you may develop an interest.

CASTING EQUIPMENT

You begin by acquiring all of the tools you'll need to cast bullets. You could go second class with some of these items, and perhaps it's good training to try out cheaper ways. You may experience some Great Livin in Grubby Times. For safety and ease of operation though, spend the extra bucks to go first class. Above all---**don't use a cheap tool if it might cause injury!**

THE MELTDOWN. Begin with something in which you can melt lead. You'll need 600° fahrenheit for pure lead and about 750° if the mixture contains antimony and tin. You might use a melting pot over a wood, gas or electric stove. When you have the mixture molten, you can use a ladle and pour the metal into a mould. Spills can occur this way, however, so be careful. We like electric bullet furnaces much better. Lee and Lyman supply good products. You get evenly controlled temperatures, plus a bottom spout for pouring right into your waiting bullet mould.

INGOT MOULDS. Ingots are large chunks of metal. Bullet casters use them as temporary storing blocks for special alloys of pre-mixed casting metal. A typical mixture would be one part tin, one part antimony, and ten parts lead. If you were to melt down lead storage battery plates, they consist of 9 to 11 parts of antimony; the rest (90 parts) of the mixture would be pure lead. That won't work for bullets. So you would add 10 to 15 parts of tin to make a good mixture, cast the ingot, and use it later as you need it.

FLUX. If you melt down most lead, tin and antimony (lighter metals) will float to the top. To keep the metals mixed, add flux---either plain beeswax or a commercial from Brownell's called Marvelux.

MOLD MALLET. You need one of these to strike and knock free the sprue cutter on a bullet mould. You can buy a commercial one, but any piece of round hard wood or plastic the size of a hammer handle will work nicely. See my book, HOW TO BE A SURVIVOR in which we show you how to make a mallet out of a tree limb. It ain't difficult. Don't use metal; it will damage the mold.

HARDNESS TESTER. You already own one; it's your fingernail. If your nail can't scratch the surface, the bullet is hard enough. Want a more accurate tester? Get a commercial one from LBT or Saeco.

THERMOMETER. Call Lyman. You need to keep track of your alloy temperatures.

BULLET MOLDS. They consist of three parts: A cavity; A sprue cutter; A wooden handle. Cavity blocks come in several sizes, from one (bullet) to a ten cavity gang mold. We recommend either a two or a four cavity mold. We also prefer aluminum over steel, even though the latter is more durable. If you go with steel, watch out for rust. *Rig* them up before storage.

That's pretty much the sum of tools you'll need. Now, let's figure out where we can scrounge free material or buy commercial stuff we can make fly out of a gun barrel.

Lead pipe, pig lead and cable sheathing consist of 100% lead. You'll need to add tin and antimony.

Linotype, lead from auto batteries, and plumber's solder also do the job. What I believe is best is the stuff I've seen "Cactus Jack" Laminack of San Diego use for years: Wheel weights. Jack put more lead into desert sand than desert turtles put droppings. But he only paid for powder and primers. He's one of the few people I know who shoots better than I. Being the shooter that he is, I figure wheel weights are best for me. Here's the mixture: One part tin, nine parts antimony, and 82 parts lead. You can purchase block tin and antimony, both of which are 100% pure. Add these by weight to get a perfect mix.

Pure lead doesn't make good bullets because it's too soft. Soft lead, even when lubed, makes more deposits in your bore than a penned up pup will drop in your living room. Eventually such deposits cause shots to go wild. So we'll make the bullets harder. We'll add 10% tin. A little antimony raises the melting point of the bullet material. That's good; we can shove a bullet down the barrel with a higher velocity and not worry about meltdown in the bore.

We recommend different mixtures for different weapons. Generally, it goes like this:

<u>Auto pistols</u>: One part tin and 10 parts lead. If you add antimony, then one part tin, one part antimony, and 20 parts lead.

<u>Revolvers</u> take a different mix: One part tin and 40 parts lead. We also like one part tin, one part antimony, and 20 parts lead.

GETTING LEAD READY TO FLY

Decide on the hardness of the bullet you'll produce. Some weapons shoot more accurately with softer bullets. Therefore, it's wise to buy a hardness tester. You can drop lead out of the mold into water to make it hard. Otherwise, drop them onto an old towel.

Fire up your furnace. Take it up to 750° and add your chosen alloy. Add a half teaspoon of flux and stir it in. Skim off any slag on the surface; it might be dirt or perhaps grease from wheel weights, etc.

Some people put their molds in an oven to preheat them because a cold mold won't produce a good bullet. Another way is to cast bullets in the mold until they come out right. Deformed bullet? Back in the pot. Later, a similar treatment will be for cooled bullets you inspect and reject due to hairline wrinkles, rounded edges, pinholes or other blemishes.

Rest your four-cavity mold on a mold guide and slide it along as you fill each sprue hole with hot lead. Each time one cavity fills, shut off the metal flow. When the alloy temperature is just right, your bullets

VARIETY OF CAST BULLETS

A   B   C

D   F   G

Upper right is C, the wadcutter. B = wadcutter with hollowed out rear. A = same but inverted to get better expansion. D = Semi-wadcutter. F = Round nose. G = Pointed bullet. This last one, G, works great when cast from pewter for .45 ACP. It comes out weighing 148 grains and speeds around 1,100 fps to puncture steel. Cast your own.

will shine like silver. Otherwise---frosted tells you the mix was too hot; wrinkled means too cool.

If you use a ladle, take melted alloy from the bottom of the pot and bring it up full. Hold your bullet mold up against the ladle with its sprue hole facing the ladle pouring spout. Now put the pouring spout into the mold's sprue hole. Holding them together, slowly rotate the mold to an upright position as the alloy pours into the mold. Stop when it's full. Repeat this method on every sprue hole.

When the alloy in the sprue hole hardens, (about 20 seconds) tap on the sprue cutter with your casting mallet to unlock the mold blocks. Open blocks; all molded bullets fall onto a cushion of old towels.

Don't forget to add flux each time you add alloy to the furnace. Tin and antimony will float to the top of the alloy mix like slag if you forget.

After producing a good number of lead bullets, we'll add gas checks. You can purchase these to stay on the bullet or fly away after the bullet leaves your barrel. Don't mix the two kinds of bullets (gas checks/ no gas checks) or you'll get some weird groups.

Since two or three grains will make a big difference down range, it's a good idea to weigh each bullet. Tongs are good for bullet handling. Weigh your bullets and keep them in separate lots according to weight.

Here's something not everyone knows: No two bores are the same diameter. If you buy ammo in a store, you get one size to fit all. If you cast bullets, you buy the mold which produces bullets to fit your bore exactly. You can measure by using "Cerrosafe" to make a casting of your bore, but it's easier to drive an oversized lead ball down your bore and measure that. Measure the casting from land to land, which is the same as muzzle measurement from groove to groove.

When you know your weapon's groove diameter, buy molds and bullet sizers to produce the bullet to fit exactly. If you can't find the one you're looking for, one or two thousandths over won't do any damage.

Lubri-size is the process by which you will force bullet lube into the bullets' grease grooves and squeeze it down to conform exactly to the bore of your individual gun. We like tapered sizing dies best, and you can get them in just about every size imaginable.

In our opinion, solid lubricants are best; get them in round stick form to fit lubri-sizers. Of course, you can also purchase liquid lubricant. You simply pour and wipe them on. After the lube dries, your bullets are ready to load. Don't load a bullet with any lube on the backside. Wipe the bullets clean. Otherwise the lube may contaminate the gun powder inside the case.

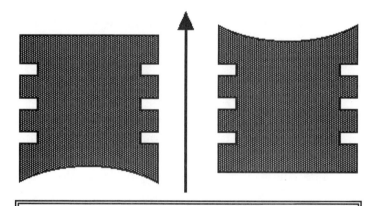

Wadcutter on left has been inverted to shoot with cup forward on the right. Note the grooves in the sides; they contain solid lube to keep the lead from fouling your barrel.

HOME MADE LUBRICANTS

Home made bullet lubricants are a good idea for the survivalist. Equal parts of paraffin and vaseline work well. You may choose to add two tablespoons of Arco brand graphite motor oil per pound of mix. Use the double boiler to blend your soup. Start with the paraffin or bees' wax first, then add vaseline. Oil goes in last. Just get it all hot enough to thoroughly blend everything together while you stir it. After it dries, you can cut it up and store it in Zip-Lock bags.

BEING PREPARED

Consider the savings. You pay for the equipment as soon as you shoot a number of rounds which would have cost the price of the equipment. After that, every bullet you cast is profit.

I have a book on the back burner called **THE GREAT RV GETAWAY,** which pretty much says you can sing "*take this job and shove it,*" and simply hit the hills. That's something I wouldn't want to do without ammo. Ammo will also be easy to sell or trade for food.

You don't have to cast and store a lot of bullets in order to be ready for a time when ammo is hard to come by. In our opinion, though, it's a skill you ought to learn. Once you've cast bullets; you've eliminated the need for heavy storage. Figure that no matter where you go, you can always find lead. With all your tools ready, powder and primers are all you need to do a whole lot of shooting for a long time.

THE HAPPY HANDGUNNER INDEX

Ambidextrous safeties 22
Attitude for combat, 120+
Ambush with handgun, "H" formation, 105
Ammunition, home made, 127; for special purposes, 133+
Authors, two, combined result, BackCover.
Basic ballistics 7
Ballistics, three kinds 7, 8
Barrel, pointed high, error of, 28; length for accuracy 68
Barricades for gunfighting, 109
BRASS system of shooting 9, 67
Bullet delivery, follow through 77, expansion after shooting, 98; cast, 141
Carry, handguns, methods 59; unconventional 60, 61; conventional 61; holsters for retrieval, 65; harness, additional uses for, 66.
Casting bullets, 141; equipment for, 142; material for, 142+
Cause of death from handgun wounds, physical 120, psycho, 120
Children in reloading area, 138
Cleaning, handgun 57
Combined authorship, benefits, 4
Cone of fire 76
Convicts, now loose because of overcrowding, 114+
Cover in gunfight 79; concealment vs cover, 116
Crimping handgun loads, 131
Dies for reloading, 131
Distance, safe shooting 30
Engagement defined, 101; misconceptions from Hollywood, 103
Equipment for reloading, 130

Exterior ballistics 8
Fire-lapping 47, 48
Force, legal use of and amount, 114
FORM, reload performance 40
Grips 51
Grips, function of 51
Grips, fitting 52
Gunfights, surprise in and speed of occurance, 109
Gun powder, burn rates, 129
Incoming, lack of information on, 114
Government, U.S., 124
Handgun, practice warning 30; choices 31+; single action 33, 34; autos 35; too much for shooter 38; rimfires 38; improvement 47; vs rifle, probable outcome, 106
Handguns, unimprovement 49
Handguns, new in box 2, 47
Hollywood, cause of fatality in gunfights, 103
Home defense, 117
Incoming fire, to handgunner 6
Index 77, 81; losing index 77
Ingot moulds, 142
Interior ballistics 7, 8
Laser sights 56
Lead fumes from casting, danger, 141
Lubricant, for cast bullets, homemade, 148
Lubrication, firearms, 36; cast bullets, 147
Magazine release buttons, mushroom 23
Marksmanship, handgun, theory 72+
Mix 'n Match, method, 11, 108, defined, 12; graph for, 14, sequence for, 16; test results from, 18; disadvantages of, 18, 19
Muzzle flash reduction, 49

Muzzle flip 7, 25
Night shooting improvements 55; flash, 91
PAUL system for level shooting 70
Partners, shooting tactics, 110; shooting in pairs, 110+; fields of fire in combat, 111
Penetrator, in magazine stack, 17; home made, 134
Perceptions, relative in combat, 116
Police firearms training, inadequacy 7, 85
Presentation 76, 81+
Press, reloading, 130
Priorities, handgun combat, 121+
Range overlap for handgun shooters 30
Reload/performance forms 5, 10; Why? 124, equipment for, 130; powder for bullet weights, 131; alcohol during, 138; source of bona fide data, 138; operational limits for firearms, 139
Safety in reloading, 137
Security, for handguns, 57; sleeping test, 107
Shooting accuracy, handgun, 21; key and methods 28; progressive learning 73+; method related to distance, 75; controlled environment 75; plan, 83+; at night, 91+
Sighting, sight methods, 32; systems, 55, 56
Sights, adjustable 10; wider rear notch 82;
Sights, adjustment for distance 29
Sizing cast bullets, 146; method of measurement for, 146

Shadows, use in tactical gunfight, 117
Shot, getting, science of, 114; result from Central Nervous System hit, 105
Shooting victims, positions, 112; how it happened, 122
Stance 78, 79
Stress, creation of for training 70
Tactics in gunfight, 116+; how to develop, 110
Target acquisition 77, 82; selection 87;
Target size, relative meaning in gunfight 71, 120
Terminal ballistics 8
Three shot group 10
Triggers 53; control of 88; methods of squeezing 89; two stage for double action, 89;
Warning shots, stupidity of, 104
Weapons, design for daylight, 55; hierarchy, 106; when matched evenly, 110; legality to carry at home, 114
Weighing powder, 131; trickler, 132
Wobble detection 4
Wobble grid 26, 27, 69
Wobble, conversion to shooting distance 69, 76
Wounds, shooting to wound, 104; from handgun, fatality, 120

GLOSSARY

ACCURIZE To make accurate. New barrel bushings, trigger jobs, custom grips and fire-lapping make handguns shoot right on target.

ACP Automatic Colt Pistol. This was the original .45 round made for the 1911 Colt auto. It's a great stopping cartridge.

AUTO Really a misnomer for a handgun which shoots each time you pull the trigger. Here, we mean "AUTO LOADER."

ANTIMONY A brittle, chemical element of crystalline structure. Used to harden metals and increase it's resistance to chemical action.

BALLISTIC COEFFICIENT A number designating how easily your bullet slices through the air.

CHAMBER Both a verb and noun. As a verb, the action of a bullet as it finds its home in front of the firing pin. As a noun, its the hollowed-out place in which a bullet rests just before firing.

CHARGE Also powder charge. Goes by weight in grains.

COCKED. Hammer back, ready to fire on handgun. See "Locked."

COEFFICIENT The number we use to designate a bullet's ability to maintain velocity after departing from the barrel.

CONCENTRIC Describes circles with same center. Without bullet-to-bore concentricity, bullets enter barrel rifling off center and flipout.

CONE OF FIRE. The measurable (irregular) circle into which your bullets fly. The size depends on your wobble, sight alignment, trigger control, and the distance you are away from your target.

CRACK. The sound a bullet makes as it passes nearby.

CRISP. Describes a trigger that snaps all of a sudden.

CYLINDER. The revolving part of a handgun which holds cartridges.

DOWN TIME. Not the happy hour; it's when your gun is empty.

DRY FIRE. To snap the trigger on an unloaded weapon. It's an excellent way of educating your trigger finger.

EXTRACTOR On the bolt face, the springy lip which grabs the spent shell casing and pulls it out of the chamber on autos.

FIRE-LAP To fire a special bullet with polishing grit and lap the bore to a mirror-smooth surface so you get early bullet stabilization.

FPE Foot Pounds of Energy. Most important at shootable range.

HOLEY Describes a target with new holes made by bullets.

INCOMING Bullets others shoot at or near you.

INTEL. Short for intelligence, it refers to all you need to know about a military or tactical situation.

LANDS AND GROOVES The spiral inside of any rifle or handgun has grooves cut into the barrel. The lands (high ridges) remain to grab the bullet and cause it to spin as it leaves the barrel.

LOCKED. Military term. Describes a weapon with the safety on.

MATCH GRADE Ammunition made with closer tolerances. Sure.

MIX 'N MATCH. Term for loading your handgun with a variety of cartridges.

MOA's Minutes of Angle. Common way we measure small arms ballistics movement. 60"=1 degree.

NOMOGRAPHIC Describes rise and fall of bullet in flight.

PERP A perpetrator of a crime.

PRE-MEDIUM MATERIAL. Target body coverings, such as heavy overcoats. Hollow points fill with that and act differently.

PRESENTATION. Act of drawing a handgun.

RANGE The distance from the shooter to a target.

RANGE OVERLAP What you get when you carry two handguns which shoot effectively from short and long distance.

RUBBING COMPOUND Brownells offers a compound paste with grit in it. In between two rough surfaces, it makes both smooth.

SAYONARA Japanese word for good-bye, frequently used by rifle shooters in long range combat against lesser weapons.

SEMI-AUTO Feeds new round into the chamber. You pull the trigger each time you fire. Automatic pistols are really semi-auto.

SHOOTABLE RANGE. The all-important distance at which you can rely on both shooter and weapon to fire and hit accurately.

SLIDE. The pistol part which comes back quickly to cock the hammer, eject a case, and then forward to seat a new round in the chamber.

SOFT POINT On a jacketed bullet, the exposed lead tip of soft material which helps the bullet to mushroom inside the target body.

STARE. Total concentration, both visual and mental on the sights of a handgun.

TAPER CRIMP. Best for autos, the sides of the brass case slim down into the bullet.

WHOMP Bullet energy at target. Same as smack, knock over, etc.

ZERO *verb and noun.* To zero your sights, you conform them so the strike of the bullet coincides with your point of aim.

ABBREVIATIONS FOR BULLET TYPES & TERMS

AP- Armor Piercing. Usually a rifle bullet. Handgun penetrators can be made at home to do a decent job. See Penetrator & Sabot.

ANNIHILATOR- A company name for a commercial handgun round which blows up when it encounters about 400 lbs resistance.

DUPLEX ROUND- Can be homemade. Generally two lead balls to match bore diameter. Also, ball & bullet combo.

FMJ-Full Metal Jacket. Bullets with lead core completely encased in jacket material, usually copper.

HB- Hollow Base. Refers to backside of wadcutters. You get a great mushroom effect if you load with hollow base in front.

HP-Hollow Point. Bullet with leading nose drilled out so that it expands in a target body.

JHP- Jacketed Hollow Point. Hollow points with a copper (other metal) jacket. The hollow point makes the diameter of the bullet expand so the smack inside the target body increases.

JSP- Jacketed Soft point.

PENETRATOR- Round designed to go through barricade. Best might be the .45 ACP round you can cast in Lyman mold out of Pewter.

RN-Round Nose. Can be either jacketed or plain lead. Shape of the bullet nose gives this round a name. Commonly used on .45 ACP ("hardball") ammunition.

SWC- Semi Wadcutter. With angle toward the nose, front of bullet is flat to achieve smack on target with penetration. LSWC=Lead semi

GAS CHECK-Small piece of jacket material behind lead bullet to keep hot gas from melting lead and fouling barrel. Also, makes a seal between gas and bullet to give better propulsion.

SABOT-French origination, therefore pronounced *sahbo.* Usually a plastic round surrounding a bullet of smaller diameter than bore size. Here, a lead bullet drilled in the center to receive a press fit of drill rod or other unusually hard steel.

SHOT SHELL. Otherwise known as snake load. Uses #12 shot and disperses a wide pattern, thus insuring a first hit on a close target.

SP- Soft Point. Bullet shape is not hollow, so air resistance isn't severe. Nevertheless, the bullet mushrooms on impact.

STHP- Silver Tip Hollow Point.

TRACER- Bullet which creates a light trail as it flies forward. Used by handgunner to signal magazine near-empty status.

WC- Wad Cutter, so named for the wad it cuts cleanly out of a paper target. The bullet is completely flat across entire diameter.

Path Finder Publications
P.O. Box 550, Kalaheo, HI 96741
Other books we publish
Tear out or copy this page and send with order.
Circle check marks for Selections

√ **THE RIFLE RULES** *Magic for the Ultimate Rifleman.*
$14.95 The ultimate! Information never before printed. Book makes you a super marksman. Hit from 900 yards+. Use our wobble grid to a never-miss, open field shot. Use our forms for ballistic perfection. Don't buy another rifle 'til you own this book.

√ **CONQUER CRIME,** *How To Be Your Own Bodyguard*
$14.95 Police can only make an arrest <u>after</u> crime has been committed. Translation: If you want their help, you first have to become a victim. Here Don investigates methods used by germs in US, hires a high-ticket bodyguard, and comes up with defenses---both tactical and practical. Keep your car un-jacked, your wife un-raped, your house un-burgled. "This book is packed with hot tips on how to beat crime." G. Gordon Liddy.

> NOTE: Don joined with a co-author for the "Forever" series. Combined, they have over 100 years of gunning experience. Dave instructed for California Highway Patrol. Don was a Green Beret.

√**CONQUER TERROR** *How To SURVIVE The Attack.* **$12.95**
How to keep poison gas out of your house. Includes plans for box to open mail and avoid bio-poisons. How to survive in your vehicle. What GUN to take with you. How to form a survival team.

√**EVERYBODY'S KNIFE BIBLE** **$12.95**. Landmark book on new, outdoor knife uses. Outdoor Life Book Club selection. *American Survival Magazine* said, "...16 of the most innovative and informative chapters on knives and knife uses ever written." Just under 30,000 now in print.

√ **EVERYBODY'S OUTDOOR SURVIVAL GUIDE.** **$12.95**. More innovations. Teaches exclusive outdoor know-how found nowhere else. Long range and defensive platform accuracy shooting. Animals for survival. Hand to hand combat, water purification, <u>plus</u> a lot more.

√ **GREAT LIVIN IN GRUBBY TIMES.** **$12.95** More advanced firearms and survival, including weapons selection and team defensive shooting. <u>Our big seller,</u> now in 3rd edition. Contains popular info from Green Beret Brian Adams on Escape and Evasion.

√ ☐ **NEVER GET LOST** *(Also known as: The Green Beret's Compass Course)* **$9.95**. Best and most simple land navigation system anywhere. We've sold over 28,000. **Throw out your maps**; go anywhere you want, then bee-line back to your starting point without having to back track. System also works equally well in darkness.

√ **24 + WAYS TO USE YOUR HAMMOCK** **$4.95** From crabtrap, to gun rest, to camouflage ghillie suit. No kidding; we really figured them out.

Use check as $2 cash. Postal money order deduct $1 more.
Add $1.50 for Shipping & Handling.

From a top cop and a Green Beret. . .

HAPPY HANDGUNNER

Pistol Power and Precision

You shouldn't buy a handgun unless you've read this book.

Not just a book---but **A HANDGUN REVOLUTION**. The current state-of-the-handgun-art is woefully deficient. The authors identify seven deadly handgun sins and correct them. For example:

Right now, 90% of the handguns in the world are loaded with only one kind of cartridge. That's **WRONG!**

Handguns are made to be shot during the day. Fix that---so they operate after dark as well.

This book enables you to make the perfect handgun choice, **PLUS** shoot with precision and speed others will never duplicate, **PLUS** secure a tactical advantage so you never get shot.

Finally, now you can copy and use our exclusive, all-new, shooters' wobble grid to develop bullet placement magic.

COLLOSAL! NOT FROM JUST ONE, BUT TWO AUTHORS WITH OVER 100 YEARS OF GUN EXPERIENCE.
From two masters who spent over one hundred years---reloading, developing new bullets and special powder loads, working as an upgrade gunsmith improving weapons, shooting in competition, teaching cops, surviving in jungles as a Green Beret, teaching snipers, carrying and shooting every conceivable kind of handgun, working as a bodyguard, shooting at night. You name it. In the gun world, one or both of these authors have been there---done that. Now they get together and teach you---how to be the ultimate handgunner.

With illustrations and photos to keep it simple. . . Certified: Quick Reader. Not literary. Created with new, exclusive concepts you can understand in a few hours.

ISBN 0-936263-30-7 $14.95